Eternal Perspective

By
Danny Karcha

The ultimate philosophical truth is this: Without Christ, all is vanity even when it's easy; with Him, all is well even when it's hard.

-Robert J. Morgan

About the Author

Danny, who was previously autistic and underweight with an IQ of 73, faced significant challenges in life. However, after a powerful encounter with God, he was healed of his autism and underweight condition, and his IQ increased to 123. Now, he is focused on discipleship, pursuing studies in ministry, and is deeply involved in Jesus Place, a ministry devoted to living fully for Jesus. Born and raised in Tacoma, Washington, Danny is passionate about theology and is committed to seeing spiritual transformation and reformation in the church, striving to spread the gospel both locally and globally.

Image Credits: Mira Redko

(Instagram: @miraredkophotoandvideo)

Contents

Introduction

Embracing the True Gospel: A Call to Genuine Relationship and Transformation

My heart is ablaze with a constant desire to live out the fundamental teachings of the Holy Bible. Why? It is because I am a devoted follower of Jesus Christ. For me, being a disciple goes beyond merely holding a belief; it entails a fervent pursuit of reflecting the very essence of Jesus in every aspect of my being—my thoughts, my words, and my acts. And Jesus wants to have a deep, intimate relationship with everyone.

Even when I have wandered from God's path, I have found comfort in the gentle embrace of His steadfast devotion. Now, I am compelled more than ever to create an opus that will demonstrate the transformative power of a life given over to the radiant love of Jesus Christ by weaving together the difficult details of my meetings, the tapestry of my faith, and the deafening echoes of His grace.

In order to rediscover the actual meaning of the Cross, I want to share my testimony in the first chapter and examine how our view of God may affect our daily lives. I want to give readers a theological perspective and a sincere message that will help them understand the real message of the Gospel.

In this book, I will discuss how to walk practically, how to produce good fruit in our lives, how to grow the body of Christ, and how to better comprehend His nature. Open and position your heart as you read this book to consider what we, as Christians, may do to advance in Christ. You can ask yourself, *"How can I grow my relationship with God more, or what can I do to get there?"* When you read scripture, you start to see the glory that comes upon you and walk in righteousness.

In the Church, we see how many, if not the majority, in the Body of Christ have missed the key to discipleship. Being a disciple simply means acting, talking, and walking like Jesus. It's recognizing that it comes with a cost that brings the joy of carrying the cross. It's building relationships with one another that Jesus has commended us to love Him with every bit of ourselves and to love our neighbor as ourselves. For some, we may hear and believe in His name just as the world knows Him, but we never give Him full access to our lives and invite Him into every area of our lives. It's important that discipleship is not the means of simply going to church once a week, but rather, it is to pursue relationships with people and God. The purpose of this book is to hit on the idea that the Gospel isn't just to go to heaven. It's not to reserve a spot because how many of us would want to go to heaven? But what if Jesus moved His position in heaven to hell? The purpose of this book is to open your eyes to see and to walk in the truth. Jesus promises that the truth will set you free.

Truth is what shapes our lives through idealism, philosophy, theism, and many worldviews. As truth may seem boring to search for, it is fundamentally important to pursue the purpose of truth. Once again, Jesus says the truth will set you free. Moses was a man who interceded on behalf of the Israelites by raising His hands up to God, holding on to the promises that God would reign in victory, and as while Moses hand became unsteady, Aaron and Her put a rock underneath him to sit and held Moses' hands up to remain steady. The truth is what helps build our foundation on the rock, Jesus. Our house, would be grounded on a rocky foundation, and as the winds, storms, and chaos came, we would be steady in His truth. Many people in the world claim they are Christians, but their bibles are hidden on their shelves, all dusted up, and they question why they are full of worry and anxiety.

Due to the prophecies, I have gotten over the years, I have felt the Lord calling me to write a book about Him. I was unable to imagine that I could write a book at the age of twenty-one (now I am 22 years old) because I had only recently reconnected with God more than a year prior. You may read this and be concerned about why I would take this step, but this kind of step was a step of faith, and I've taken the time with the Lord and through leaders that poured into me.

I can present to you this book that will impact you and also encourage you to step out of your faith and see Jesus, who wants to build a deeper relationship with you. This project is an act of faith. I was the seed sown on rough, thorny soil when I first encountered the Lord when I was sixteen years old. My heart wasn't in the proper position. I vacillated between living for the world and Him for years as a result. Because I lacked a firm base, the raging seas frequently carried me off the intended course. I knew the Lord but didn't *know* Him. You may know the president of the United States, but you don't know him *personally.*

I want to deliver what the Bible says about our walk in Christ. In what practical ways can we fulfill the call of God in our lives or what He wants us to do? What does the Bible say about walking in the Gospel? We live in a wicked world, but Christ will ultimately and always reign in victory. It's only through the blood of Jesus that we wash every part of our lives, and it's a continually occurring process of sanctification that makes us walk more freely. You can accomplish the will of God but remain in a place of complacency and idleness.

God isn't a person who withdraws Himself because the world is too messed up to clean up. There has been much evidence of revival that has been documented for many decades. Revival is an outpouring of His Spirit that happened many times in the Old Testament and even in the early church, when the one hundred twenty in the upper room were filled by the Holy Ghost. God is more intentional with us than any man in the world. He is waiting for us to submit ourselves to Him and lose our lives to receive His life. He is not just a Creator, but a Father who is above His Creator's nature and title. Revival is born when people are willing to receive the power of the Holy Spirit and fire, and it's a byproduct of seeking Jesus. We don't look for what Jesus can offer; we look at Him for who He is. Hunger looks like something. No matter the circumstances that may arise in our lives, Christ has died for us so that we can inherit His life in us. His status was given up to go low as a baby, a bondservant, and he humbled Himself to the point of death, even death on the Cross (see Philippians 2:7-9). It is beholding the One who was slain in that He would receive the reward of His suffering.

Most importantly, please do not look at this book as your main book to guide you; those born-again, allow the Holy Spirit to speak to you in this book. Not to look at your understanding but His understanding. As I said, the main goal is that we become disciples of Jesus, not just believers, and we are called to walk into that biblically. In its simplest terms, discipleship is learning to walk, talk, and act like Jesus. I want to encourage you that there is a difference between a believer and a disciple of Jesus.

Jesus did not come to die for you, but to reconcile and to have a relationship with you.

Chapter 1: Who is He?

The Challenge of Believing in Jesus and Bearing Fruit

Now, for many of us, we have understood that Jesus is someone who has died, been buried, and been resurrected. We agree that He's done this for us to make covenants with Him and give us access to the life of Jesus. However, your perspective on Jesus will determine how you walk with God. A Calvinist person may preach the same gospel as an Armenian person. They both believe in Jesus; they desire to preach the gospel, but theologically, they are slightly different. In this case, it's okay if people have different theological stances, as long as we remain true to what the Bible says. However, to go a step further, one can preach the gospel like an orphan who begs people to come to God with an awful tone, and the other can preach the gospel with sincerity and purity as a son who walks in their identity in Christ. This is the problem. There are a variety of scenarios in which people preach the gospel for different motives. We don't preach the gospel out of unhealthy fear or for personal gain; rather, we are witnesses. A witness is someone who has experienced the goodness of God that has changed their life. Now I want you, as the reader, without theologically and biblically, ask Jesus, *"Who are You to me?"* I want you to take a second and really think about the characteristics of God and ask what those characteristics mean to you.

To me, Jesus is patient, kind, sweet, and simple, yet he came with power and a sword to bring forth righteousness on earth. A lot of times, and I can say this myself to be vulnerable, but I've seen in myself and in others that we positioned ourselves as slaves or orphans. Jesus does *not* see us that way, which is why I used John 15:13–15 as a scripture example that Jesus sees us as friends. Why are we to act like slaves or orphans if Jesus says otherwise? He is too kind and meek for us to be His slaves; it doesn't make sense. You see, I believe we see how many times we position ourselves in areas that God doesn't want us to be in. Whether it's being in a financial situation, being disappointed that God didn't heal a physical injury, or feeling like he's not close to us, the issue in the church today is that we see Jesus as someone distant, when instead, He continually prays and intercedes for us every single second, both to believers and unbelievers. He wants people to come to know Him as our loving Father. He's thinking about us every second and wants us to speak with Him. You may wonder why people would think that God is distant, but according to Gnosticism, which began in the 5th century, 1/3 of the Church population was rooted in Gnosticism and believed that the spiritual was good but the natural world was bad. In other words, theology shapes the way we view God. God is a person who came down fully man and fully God and who wants us to be with Him.

Later on in this chapter, I will go over one verse to break down the characteristics of God according to the Hebrew authors. Many other people outside of the church (and those who don't have an authentic, fruitful Christian lifestyle) *know* who Jesus is because it is something many cultures hear. If you think about it, I believe ninety-nine percent of people in the world have heard of Jesus. It's someone with whom we are familiar but don't know Him personally. Maybe Jesus is someone you grew up with because your family goes to church. Even many other religions know Jesus was on Earth but do not believe He is the Son of God—Christians who have grown up in the Church are familiar with the stories in the Gospel. Our theology and our experiences shape our view of who God is. Can it be that many people, due to their worldviews, have misunderstood who God truly is according to the Bible?

You can believe in heaven, but not in the Son of God. It's not in the sense of work-based salvation; this isn't the motive I'm picturing, but rather, how can one person invite the God of the universe who wants to help the person in life? Who helped out Moses when He divided the sea and led the Israelites out of Egypt? A correlation between Moses and Jesus is that Jesus is the new Moses according to His nature as the Savior and how His birth is similar to what Moses has gone through as a baby. Pharaoh wanted to kill every son (Exodus 1:22), while King Herod was also trying to kill every male baby under two years old as Joseph and Mary fled from Bethlehem (Matthew 2:16). It's beautiful when you start to see the way God designed the Bible.

I speak to those who may not understand who God is as a Father, who is very intentional to us even when we don't see it. As I said, you can accomplish the will of God but miss the potential God has for your life. You can have the title of 'Christian' and completely forget the power of His Word in your life. Let me share the deity of Jesus Christ from John 1 and Genesis 1 to cross-reference:

In the beginning, God created the heavens and the earth. The earth was formless and void; darkness was over the deep surface; and the Spirit of God was moving over the surface of the waters. Then God said, "Let there be light," and there was light. God saw that the light was good, and God separated the light from the darkness. God called the light day and the darkness night. And there was evening, and there was morning, one day. (Genesis 1:1-5)

In the beginning was the Word, and the Word was with God, and the Word was God. He was in the beginning with God. All things came into being through Him; apart from Him, nothing came into being that has come into being. In Him was life, and life was the Light of men. The Light shines in the darkness, and the darkness did not comprehend it. (John 1:1-5)

John pictured and pointed out to many of us that he was a witness to the glory that was manifested in the Son. If the Word of God *is* Him, why don't people see Him that way? The Word made in the flesh is the Word we read in our Bibles. Jesus *is* the Word from the beginning, before creation was ever created. Notice how the word *'light'* plays in these two passages—a light that *consumes* darkness, including our lives. The light is good and pleasing to Him. He wants to bring light into you. The Bible is a love letter from God.

The essence of the Gospel is not solely about receiving Jesus Christ to secure eternal life with Him. It goes beyond a transactional agreement or contract-like covenant; instead, it is fundamentally rooted in establishing a deep and intimate relationship with God. While some may perceive the Gospel as a contractual arrangement wherein one gains the right to enter heaven by simply reciting a sinner's prayer, the true essence of a Christian's life extends far beyond that initial moment. It encompasses the ongoing journey of discipleship and stewardship, which can significantly impact the fruitfulness and transformation of one's life.

In many instances, the recitation of the sinners' prayer can be seen as an indispensable step towards Salvation. However, it should not be perceived as the ultimate goal or the end of the Christian journey. The sinner's prayer is a gateway, an entry point, to begin a relationship with God through Jesus Christ. It is an acknowledgment of one's need for a Savior and a declaration of faith in Jesus as that Savior. Similarly, as in marriage.

However, it is crucial to understand that this decision you make is the beginning of a lifelong journey of faith and growth in Christ.

The danger could arise if discipleship and stewardship are not prioritized and the sinners' prayer is seen as the only requirement for a connection with God. Learning, developing, and maturing in Jesus Christ's teachings and ways are all parts of discipleship. Studying and putting the Bible's teachings into practice, seeking the Holy Spirit's direction, and evolving into Christ's image are all ongoing processes. All in having a relationship with Him.

On the other hand, stewardship refers to the responsible management and use of the gifts, talents, resources, and opportunities that God has entrusted to us. It is about recognizing that everything we have is a gift from God and using those gifts and resources for His glory and the benefit of others.

"that He would grant you, according to the riches of His glory, to be strengthened with power through His Spirit in the

inner man, so that Christ may dwell in your hearts through faith; and that you, being rooted and grounded in love, may be able to comprehend with all the saints what is the breadth and length and height and depth, and to know the love of Christ which surpasses knowledge, that you may be filled up to all the fullness of God." (Ephesians 3:16-19)

When someone solely relies on the sinners' prayer without actively pursuing discipleship and stewardship, their relationship with God can become stagnant and unfruitful. The lack of ongoing growth and transformation can lead to a life marked by bondage to sin, spiritual immaturity, and a limited experience of the abundant life that Jesus promises.

Here, we must recognize that a genuine relationship with God is not based solely on a one-time prayer. Nevertheless, it is an ongoing commitment to follow Jesus, seek His will, and allow His transformative power to work in our lives. Through cultivating this relationship, nourished by discipleship and stewardship, we can experience the fullness of God's love, grace, and transformative power.

Now, I am not against the sinner's prayer, it's an act of repentance. I believe it's important to lead an unbeliever to repentance, especially if they are unsure how to invite Him in. I believe many have missed our goodness and rewarding covenant and left God out of the picture. It is heartbreaking that people don't see Him as a Father but as some distant cosmic being with whom we can't have an authentic relationship.

The Roman Empire influenced many people in the day when Christianity was born. And with the Greek perspective of seeing the truth with logic and belief, we miss what the Eastern Christians (Hebraic/Jewish view) actually viewed God as: a Father, a Provider (Yahweh Jirah), a Healer (Yahweh Healer), and many more Yahweh titles. He is a God who wants to bless us only through our trust in Him. We have to be transformed by the Word. Not adding our beliefs to the Word, but allowing the Word to change our beliefs.

With logic and understanding of God, people tend to be more resilient on the things of the secular and exclude the invitation of God, due to a belief that He is separate from the natural realm. God knows everything about you and what's happening, but He wants you to invite Him into those moments. He cares for the tiniest details in your life.

Now, I said I'd go over two verses in the Bible that describe the nature of God. I encourage you that, in order to see Him, we have to put away how people and culture describe the nature of God. Although the nature of God is a huge subject on its own, in this chapter, we will go over one verse that describes Him very well. We will take a look at the book of Exodus when Moses went to Mount Sinai the second time after the Israelites worshipped the golden calf and broke the ten commandments.

6 Then the Lord passed by in front of him and proclaimed, "The Lord, the Lord God, compassionate and gracious, slow to anger, and abounding in lovingkindness and truth; 7 who keeps lovingkindness for thousands, who forgives iniquity, transgression, and sin; yet He will by no means leave the guilty unpunished, visiting the iniquity of fathers on the children and on the grandchildren to the third and fourth generations." (Exodus 34:6-7 NASB95)

Notice these two verses reveal the five characteristics of God: a Father who looks out for His children but is also a just God. I will break down the five characteristics to reveal how the Hebrew authors describe God.

Compassionate:

The first characteristic of God is 'compassionate.' The Hebrew word for this is 'rachûwm' (rakh-oom'), also known as 'Rekhem' meaning "Womb." The Hebrew authors describe this as imagining a mother's tender feelings towards her baby child. In other words, 'Rakhum' conveys intense emotion or is "deeply moved," but it's not just an emotional word; it's also an action word. An example of this is when Solomon wisely judged the two women who both tried to claim that this one baby was their child after one of their sons had died, yet believed their own baby is still alive.

24 And the king said, "Get me a sword." So they brought a sword before the king. 25 And the king said, "Cut the living child in two, and give half to one and half to the other." 26 But the woman whose child was the living one spoke to the king, for she was deeply stirred over her son, and she said, "Pardon me, my lord! Give her the living child, and by no means kill him!" But the other woman was saying, "He shall be neither mine nor yours; cut him!" 27 Then the king replied, "Give the first woman the living child, and by no means kill him. She is his mother." (1 Kings 3:24–27)

The real mother of the baby is deeply moved; she would much rather see her baby live than die. Now you may look at the bold text in this small passage, this was my intention. Do you see the gospel behind this? Imagine our Father, who was deeply moved by our brokenness; rather than for us to suffer in our sin and experience death, we can get to witness Jesus dying for us. The Father created us in His image, which reveals our identity in Christ. It's out of His Rekhem (compassion) that He was always providing and serving us, just like the Israelites after Egypt were always provided with food, water, and clothing. Yet, despite His compassion and provision, the Israelites still chose to turn away and reject God's compassion and choose to give their allegiance to other idols, violence, and darkness. In even the darkest moments, the prophet Isaiah wrote this as a reminder that, although maybe even our earthly mothers and fathers have failed us, our Father will never forget us.

15: "Can a woman forget her nursing child and have no compassion for the son of her womb? Even these may forget, but I will not forget you. (Isaiah 49:15)

God is full of motherly compassion and rescues His people by becoming a deeply compassionate baby and raising them by serving others, such as the sick and the lost. Jesus compares Himself to a mother hen using her wings to shield her chicks as He gathers people into His embrace. The Greek word for compassion is *Oiktirmos*; He gave His ultimate expression of *Oiktirmos* by entering into humanity's suffering and being willing to die for us, rescuing us, and bringing us back near to God. Now, by accessing Him by faith, we too can imitate Him and be moved by the compassion of Jesus. We learn this by looking at the model of discipleship of Jesus—how He blessed His enemies, served, loved, took care of the poor and widows, and gave many examples of deep humility. In the words of Jesus, He says this:

"36: Be compassionate just as your Father is compassionate." (Luke 6:36 CEB)

Gracious:

The second characteristic of God we will look at is 'gracious.' The Hebrew word for this is 'channûwn' (khan-noon'), meaning that it's a favor or gift. Another Hebrew word that connects to this is 'khen' meaning delightful or favorable. In the book of psalms, you can describe the psalmist writing and singing the songs with delight, who has the lips of khen that sound gracious. *"You are fairer than the sons of men; grace is poured upon your lips. Therefore, God has blessed you forever. (Psalms 45:2)* In other words, the psalmist can craft beautiful words that delight those who hear the songs. When we allow ourselves to meditate on God's words and His delight towards us, we hear Him just like the Psalmist, who speaks life into us. Or, if we look at Jesus and behold what He has done for us, He is similar to a shiny ornament that we delight in. Just like we see that grace is a gift, we see Jesus as a gift from our Heavenly Father with delight and favor. If we fail to look back at our precious gift, we are reminded that God is gracious towards us and that He will never stop pursuing us and that we should continue to follow Him. We can also ask for God's grace and favor regarding our finances, healing, ministering to others, and loving others; in anything we can ask for, He favors us and grants us our wishes.

As in the book of Esther. We see that Esther, in chapter 8, fell at King Ahasuerbus's feet and asked if he would avert the evil scheme of Haman that he plotted against the Jews, and the king extended the golden scepter to Esther and found favor in her and gave her the house of Haman. The King found delight in Esther. How about Jacob? After twenty years of Jacob betraying and leaving Esau, he decided to return, and although he should have deserved punishment and feared Esau, he asked Esau for a favor. Jacob bowed down seven times, showing humility and repentance toward Esau. And in Esau's response, Esau runs to meet him, embraces him, and weeps. Now with God, His greatest gift was sending His Son, someone who would be a blessing to anyone, to those who received this Gift.

31 What then shall we say to these things? If God is for us, who is against us? 32 He who did not spare His own Son but delivered Him over for us all, how will He not also with Him freely give us all things? (Romans 8:31-32) Jesus was a man we should have never deserved, and He decided to step in and freely give Himself so we could be with our Father. We learn that through Him, we can also give grace to those who shouldn't deserve punishment, but rather, to lift up one another out of His love for us.

Slow to Anger:

The third characteristic we will look at is 'slowness of anger', which in Hebrew is 'erek 'appayim.' (Meaning: long of nose). What does God's patience have to do with a long nose? According to Jewish metaphors, when you are angry or get heated, your nose is the first thing that heats up and then your entire face heats up. One common biblical story is when someone is angry; their nose is burned hot.

19 Now when his master heard the words of his wife, which she spoke to him, saying, "This is what your slave did to me," <u>his anger burned.</u> 20 So Joseph's master took him and put him into the jail, the place where the king's prisoners were confined; and he was there in the jail. 21 But the Lord was with Joseph, extended kindness to him, and gave him favor in the sight of the chief jailer. 22 The chief jailer committed to Joseph's charge all the prisoners who were in the jail; so that whatever was done there, he was responsible for it. 23 The chief jailer did not supervise anything under Joseph's charge because the Lord was with him, and whatever he did, the Lord made to prosper. (Genesis 39:19-23)

The main words for anger in Hebrew are Nose or Heat, or Hot Nose. This is why a patient person is called "Long of Nose." It takes them a long time for their nose to get hot, like in the biblical proverb, where a wise and patient man is described as someone who has a 'long of nose.' Proverbs 19:11 says: **11** A man's discretion makes him slow to anger, and it is his glory to overlook a transgression."

A person's wisdom is their long nose. Although God doesn't have a long nose, it's a metaphor for God's patience toward injustice and evil in the world. Similarly, if you saw someone who was getting bullied in a playground, you would get angry. God gets angry when humans oppress each other. His anger expresses His justice and His love for the world. He's slow to anger and gives lots of time for people to change. Like Pharaoh, who enslaved the Israelites when thrown into the waters, God responded by using someone like Moses, giving them ten chances to surrender. Pharaoh burst with anger, trying to capture the Israelites through the Red Sea, and God destroyed him in the waters. The Pharaoh's evil turned back against him.

"And in the greatness of Your excellence, You overthrow those who rise up against You; You send forth Your burning anger, and it consumes them as chaff. (Exodus 15:7)

Throughout the scriptures, there's always a pattern where, whenever the Israelites betray God into worshipping other gods, He will respond by giving them what they want, which are other nations that come in and defeat Israel. Apostle Paul even says in Romans that God allowed people to have their own destructive desires and decisions, even if they led to death. I'd highly encourage you to read Romans 1:18–32 for context. To simplify it, God reveals His judgment against all the ungodliness and wickedness of people who suppress the truth. Despite knowing God through His creation, they chose not to honor Him and turned to idolatry. As a result, God allowed them to follow their sinful desires, leading to moral decay and various sins. This passage highlights God's justice in letting people face the consequences of their deliberate rejection of Him and their wrongdoing. The next chapter of Romans, also reveals that God's kindness leads people to repentance. Giving people time to come to their senses and change.

1 Therefore you have no excuse, everyone of you who passes judgment, for in that which you judge another, you condemn yourself; for you who judge practice the same things. 2 And we know that the judgment of God rightly falls upon those who practice such things. 3 But do you suppose this, O man, when you pass judgment on those who practice such things and do the same yourself, that you will escape the judgment of God? 4 Or do you think lightly of the riches of His kindness, tolerance, and patience, not knowing that the kindness of God leads you to repentance? (Romans 2:1-4)

Remember, God's anger is a response to human evil, God is not content to allow people to sit in their own self-destruction. It's the reason we see that, although God forgives thousands, he won't declare the guilty innocent.

"Who keeps loving kindness for thousands, who forgives iniquity, transgression, and sin; yet He will by no means leave the guilty unpunished, visiting the iniquity of fathers on the children and on the grandchildren to the third and fourth generations." (Exodus 34:7)

We see that although sin may influence the third and fourth generations, His love for us is far greater. We know what's wrong. If you have been walking with the Lord for a while, you know that pornography or lying is a sin. Pretty obvious, but due to sin blinding people, it's difficult to receive breakthroughs because many people have forgotten the truth that will see them free. Which is why Jesus came in to rescue us and went to Jerusalem to die, demonstrating His love towards His enemies by taking the consequences of man upon Himself. When God is angry and brings justice, it's because He's good and extremely patient and works out His plan to restore people to His love. He's a Father who loves to take care of us, and He wants us to run to Him for any mistakes we have made.

Lovingkindness:

The next characteristic we will go over is 'lovingkindness', also known as 'loyal love', and in Hebrew it's cheçed (kheh'-sed). Lovingkindness is also known as "loyal love," and we can recognize that while most of our experiences involve betrayal and misfortune, God has loyal love that abounds. It's difficult to translate into different languages because it combines the ideas of love, generosity, and enduring commitment into one. Khesed describes an act of promise-keeping loyalty motivated by deep personal care, similar to compassion or 'Rakhum', a loving mother who is motivated by compassion and remains loyal to her baby. An example is in the story of Ruth, a foreign woman married to an Israeli man. Tragically, her husband dies along with his brother and father, and all she has left is her widowed mother-in-law, Naomi. Naomi encouraged Ruth to go back to her family, but Ruth insisted on staying by Naomi's side and taking care of her.

10 *Then he said, "May you be blessed by the Lord, my daughter. You have shown your last kindness (Khesed) to be better than the first by not going after young men, whether poor or rich. (Ruth 3:10)*

Ruth's khesed (lovingkindness) is not conditional love; it's her actions that reveal what kind of heart Ruth carries, not because of her works but because of who she is. It's an expression of Ruth's character; she is just a generous and loving person. Similarly, we see Jesus as someone who is generous (khen) and a loving person. He always keeps His Word, such as in Deuteronomy, that He will never leave us, forsake us, or fail us. His promises are true and will never go void. God has the most enduring Khesed in the Bible. What about Jacob, a person who is a liar even to his own family, but despite that, God still chooses him because of the covenant his grandfather, Abraham, has made and repeats the promise of having a huge family and being a blessing to the nations? Oftentimes, how much do we forget the promises and the goodness we have in Christ because of our mistakes? Even Jacob, after twenty years of running, realized how undeserving he was. He said to God, I am not worthy of the Khesed you have shown me.

"**10** I am unworthy of all the lovingkindness (Khesed) and of all the faithfulness which You have shown to Your servant; for with my staff *only* I crossed this Jordan, and now I have become two companies." (Genesis 32:10)

"**4** Then Esau ran to meet him, embraced him, fell on his neck, and kissed him, and they wept." (Genesis 33:4-11)

God's Khesed was not about Jacob's worth in the first place; it's a display of God's generous loyalty to his promise. Jesus doesn't want to see your works or your worth; He just loves you because He loves you. God remembers the promise to Abraham and Jacob when the Israelites were in Egypt, and He defeated Egypt, raised Moses, and liberated the people. It's about God keeping to His word. However, afterward, due to fear in the wilderness, people doubted God's loyal love and protection. They decided to threaten Moses and appoint a new leader to bring people back to Egypt. Moses steps in and says to God:

Numbers 14:19

19 *"Pardon, I pray, the iniquity of this people according to the greatness of Your lovingkindness, just as You also have* *forgiven this people from Egypt even until now." (Numbers 14:19)*

Moses asked God to forgive the people not because they deserved it but because it was consistent with God's character. It's God for who He is. Of course, He wants people to respond with Khesed, but even if they don't, His Khesed remains, and it endures. Psalm 136 is all about Khesed. This repeats 26 times that His Khesed is forever. God still kept His promise dramatically and drastically by becoming human and binding himself to us in the person of Jesus. Jesus is the ultimate loyal and loving human. Through His life, death, and resurrection, He opened up a new future for all of us and for all of creation. God did this because that's who He is: generous, loving, and eternally loyal to His promises. And now, we can experience the purity and power of God's loyal love shown through Jesus; it compels us and teaches us how to show loyal love towards us.

Truth:

Lastly, the fifth and final characteristic of God according to Exodus 34:6 is truth, also known in Hebrew ('emeth). Sound familiar? It's how we say 'Amen' to God. Which is an untranslated Hebrew expression that means "that's truth."

Emet can mean truth or refer to correct ideas and concepts. It has to do with stability and reliability. This is why our lens can determine how we view truth when we look carefully at the scriptures. For example, Moses put his hands up for hours, shaking in instability, and interceded on behalf of Israel to defeat the Amalekites. His friends put a rock under him and supported his hands so that they would remain steady.

Similarly, His truth sets us free and builds a foundation that will not be shaken or unsteady. When emet is used to describe people, it speaks of them as stable and trustworthy. For example, when Moses appointed leaders in Israel, they were to be people of emet, trustworthy people. Those who wouldn't bring injustice.

"**21** Furthermore, you shall select out of all the people able men who fear God, men of truth, and those who hate dishonest gain; and you shall place *these* over them *as* leaders of thousands, of hundreds, of fifties, and of tens." (Exodus 18:21)

God is faithful and trustworthy; Moses calls God a rock, faithful, just, and upright. Moses can trust God because of His consistency in character.

The verb in Emet is "He'emin" and can be translated as "to believe," "to have faith," or "to trust." Abraham was an example of a trustworthy person. God promised Abraham and Sarah that they would have a huge family and that through them, all nations would experience God's blessing. Despite being barren, Abraham still trusted the promise. As the stories go by, the Israelites feared God until other nations, such as the giants with giant cities, lost their faith in God. David trusted God when he faced the giants because of his emet towards God and his trust in Him.

6 Then Solomon said, "You have shown great lovingkindness to Your servant David my father, according as he walked before You in **truth (emet)** *and righteousness and uprightness of heart toward You; and You have reserved for him this great* *lovingkindness, that You have given him a son to sit on his throne, as it is this day. (1 Kings 3:6)*

16 "Your house and your kingdom shall endure before Me forever; your throne shall be established forever."'" (2 Samuel 7:16)

This faithful king will become the source of trust and stability for others forever. Even after many troubles and destructions that were brought to the Israelites, many have doubted God's promises to Abraham and David. Is God trustworthy and faithful to us? The lineage of Jesus reveals that He is the son of David and the son of Abraham.

Now that we have finished our overview of Exodus 34:6, we see the Father's nature and how He operates and takes care of us. He's a Father who takes care of us with compassion, is gracious, abounds in lovingkindness, and speaks truth to us as we are His sons and daughters, but we are not done just yet. Let's go quickly to Genesis 3:

8 They heard the sound of the Lord God walking in the garden in the cool of the day, and the man and his wife hid themselves from the presence of the Lord God among the trees of the garden. 9 Then the Lord God called to the man, and said to him, "Where are you?" 10 He said, "I heard the sound of You in the garden, and I was afraid because I was naked; so I hid myself." 11 And He said, "Who told you that you were naked? Have you eaten from the tree of which I commanded you not to eat?" (Genesis 3:8-11)

You may know the story about Adam and Eve and how they ate the forbidden fruit. Notice here that God's approach to the two wasn't out of anger, but if you look closely in verse 11, it says that God asked Adam, "Who told you that you were naked." In other words, what kind of lie are you believing that wasn't from Me? Many of us have experienced lies that aren't from God Himself. It's sad that we live in a world where we mistake the truth for a lie.

In the beginning, God created the Garden so He could have total intimacy with Adam and Eve. It's one of the biggest stories in the Bible; however, I believe many don't know the context behind the story. It's the most common story in the Bible, but I believe many are unaware of the context. The reason being that most people see God as an angry God as a response to Adam's sin or that Adam became evil and then ate the fruit of his own free will.

Most of the views carried in the world believe that Adam and Eve willingly rebelled against God; however, it's important to dig deep and carefully discern the text that Adam and Eve were *deceived*, not willingly *choose* to sin (see Genesis 3:12-13).

How can Adam and Eve sin willingly when they were perfect in all ways?

The Promise of Redemption and the Victory of Jesus

The scripture provided to us is as straightforward as it says that Eve was the one who was deceived by the serpent (see Genesis 3:13), and Adam ate the fruit willingly. One of the saddest stories is that fear came upon Adam and Eve. It wasn't because God would strike them down with lightning, but because they realized they were naked after eating the fruit of the knowledge of good and evil. God wanted to restore the intimacy between the two they once had. They spiritually died, and their perfect intimacy was destroyed and separated from God (see Genesis 3:8–10). The tree wasn't ready; they ate too soon, and Adam possibly ate the fruit so that he could be with Eve. There are many interpretations of the story.

The first good news of Jesus' return is in Genesis, also known as *'Proto-Evangelium.'* ('First good news' in Greek.) In Genesis 3:14–16, it says:

"The Lord God said to the serpent,

"Because you have done this,

Cursed are you more than all cattle,

And more than every beast in the field;

On your belly, you will go,

And dust you will eat

All the days of your life;

And I will put enmity

Between you and the woman,

And between your seed and her seed;

He shall bruise you on the head,

And you shall bruise him on the heel."

To the woman, He said,

"I will greatly multiply

Your pain in childbirth,

In pain, you will bring forth children;

Yet your desire will be for your husband,

And he will rule over you."

(Genesis 3:14–16, NASB 1995)

God cursed the serpent; the first promise of the Messiah is that God puts enmity between the women and the serpent. Those who are of the seed of the women would follow God, and they would be in favor of God until Christ came back. On the other hand, the serpent's seed represents wicked people who would bruise the heel of humanity with sin, sickness, and death. Ultimately, Christ will crush and conquer the head by taking Himself to the Cross.

A symbol to look at is that Jesus would be bitten by the serpent, taking all the sin, sickness, and death, and Jesus crushing the serpent's head instantly. Jesus defeated death when He resurrected (see 1 Corinthians 15:54–55). The Gospel brings power to those who call upon the name of the Lord. Jesus was a perfect man who knew no sin, to be sin on our behalf so that we might become the righteousness of God (see 2 Corinthians 5:21).

His ultimate act of love was demonstrated on the Cross, where He willingly sacrificed Himself for our sins, even when we were still lost in our transgressions. Sin, in its essence, is a separation from God, and it holds no hierarchy; every form of sin holds equal weight. Regrettably, sin brings about death and corrupts our spirit, soul, and body. We, believers, have received the gift of righteousness from God to be right-standing with Him (see Romans 5:17). Romans 10:9 says:

"That if you confess with your mouth Jesus as Lord, and believe in your heart that God raised Him from the dead, you will be saved."

It is a daily decision to believe in and follow Jesus after receiving Salvation. To choose Him rather than our own. To rely on Him more than ourselves. It's a partnership, but not a covenant. A relational covenant. His cross is the covenant that is available to us.

Personal Testimony: From Brokenness to Freedom: A Journey of Transformation and Purpose

Before you continue reading this book, I would like to share my personal testimony. I was born into a conservative Slavic family in Tacoma, Washington, along with my parents and three siblings. During my early years, I received a diagnosis of moderate autism. This diagnosis encompassed various challenges, such as difficulties in both receptive and expressive language, social interactions, and pervasive developmental abnormalities. Throughout my life, I faced numerous obstacles due to my struggles with communication, which made it challenging for me to connect with others and form friendships. Social interactions and speech posed the biggest barriers to finding companionship; I could only establish friendships if others reached out to me. It wasn't until the second grade that I was finally able to make friends. I attended speech therapy twice a week after school to improve my communication skills.

In addition to these challenges, I also dealt with various health issues related to my early underweight, including constipation, stomach problems, and eating disorders. Despite being raised in a Church environment throughout my entire life, the name Jesus was unfamiliar to me until later on.

Because of how my friends treated me, I became conscious of who I was, and I developed self-hatred. I wouldn't say that I loved who I was or didn't enjoy how I acted or talked. Every time I made a mistake or even just bought the lie that I did something, even if it wasn't my fault, I'd make myself hard to forgive. At the age of fourteen, when I was in middle school, I was exposed to watching porn. I developed an addiction to it, and it was one of the biggest fortifications the enemy had built. I had no empathy, was stoic, and had no interest in worldly things.

Don't get me wrong, my life wasn't that terrible, but it's not holy, and I would have gone to hell if I never believed in Jesus, I'll be real with myself. I was creative. I used to write a few ten-page comics as a kid. I was gifted in my intellect and would mostly hang out with the general education kids in elementary school. There were ups and downs, but in my middle school years, I didn't care much for school. I was pretty overweight— just as I mentioned about my eating disorders. I used to be very skinny, and I suddenly became very overweight.

I took a general IQ exam in my sophomore year to update my SPED results, and I recall scoring below average, between 75 and 79. During the academic year, it seemed embarrassing, and I was unable to discuss it with anyone else. We grew rather close, and I used to have a big crush on this girl from middle school. I was eventually duped into believing she liked me. We used to be really close, but when I learned she had a boyfriend, it broke my heart. Never in my life have I felt so emptiness.

Around that same time, at sixteen years old, I hadn't met the Lord until May 2018. In other words, I never had that raw encounter with the Lord. I know Jesus but haven't personally met the man. I went to this teen bible school program my mom forced me to attend, which was the end of my sophomore year, and one night there was an altar call.

I had the impression that I was being guided to the alter rather than having my own two feet carry me there. I sat there motionless for thirty seconds on my own two knees. Next to me, one of the leaders approached and inquired as to what he might pray for. Before the Holy Spirit unexpectedly descended upon me, and I immediately fell on my face, this leader had never placed hands on me in prayer or done anything else.

That moment, I supernaturally encountered Jesus for the first time, and it was then that I truly accepted Him. I heard the audible voice of God of Him saying, *"Let go."* It was then that the Holy Spirit was revealed to me, accompanied by the evidence of tongues. Not only that, but I was delivered (or healed) from autism, eating disorders, self-hatred, et cetera.

Freeing me from all sickness, I was accepted by the Lord with open arms. I was the kind of seed whose roots didn't develop well when planted on rock-hard ground. *Now, this is why discipleship is vital in the body.* Here's why:

After the Holy Acceptance, I had a honeymoon phase with the Lord for two weeks. The divine period after meeting Him was when I felt content and complete. However, it was short-lived, and my feelings and efforts toward him soon became lukewarm. I didn't care about the Lord too much. My motivation as a Christian was to secure my Salvation, but the lifestyle wasn't it. I lived fifty-fifty for the world and Him. The lifestyle I had at the time wasn't the most fruitful. Pornography came back into my life; I would be around harmful or toxic people and drink and smoke occasionally, but I lacked the reverence of the Lord.

I had no idea how much my mind was expanding academically. In high school, I made significant academic gains overall. I switched from taking one each of math, English, and reading in three of the six SPED subjects I had my freshman year. I completed my senior year with all general education courses as well as two AP courses in computer science and English. I purchased these packets of edibles that contained large quantities of THC, perhaps 1000 mg, as COVID-19 began, moving forward toward the graduation year of 2020. I took them in the summer of 2020, shattering my understanding of both the world and God.

Trying to decide which college to go to, what branch of the military I felt like joining, etc., I fell so much into the world that I accomplished nothing for the past year. As I filled myself with worldly possessions and stopped going outside, working, or doing anything else, I grew away from the Lord. It served no purpose. I suddenly wanted to stop watching porn around May 2021 after coming back from a youth leadership program. I became aware of how significantly it would impact my upcoming friendships, partnerships, marriages, etc. In the summer of 2021, I was trying to kick this addiction while being self-righteous, and every time I stumbled, I would feel so guilty, so ashamed, and so condemned.

I began reading my Bible and being intentional with the Lord around September and October of 2021, hoping He would set me free. Because I've witnessed the effects of healing, deliverance, and liberation in other people's lives, such as in my ministry in Seattle called *'Jesus Place.'* I believe that if they can find freedom, then so can I. I also experienced His calm each time I read the Bible. I'd finish reading my Bible and put it away, and I'd have terrible worry the rest of the day. Without understanding it, I was experiencing demonic dominance throughout those two months. The lies of my history were being served by the enemy, and I was experiencing more fear than I had as an unsaved, damaged child.

After one of the most difficult struggles of my life, around November 2021, my older cousin asked me to attend this large Church service. I attended this event where everyone was fervently pursuing the Gospel. I spent the first hour in worship and longed to be set free. While I was in the midst of praying, a friend of mine, Aliyah, approached me and asked if she could pray for me. Aliyah asked if she could hold my forearms. I gave her my arms, and she grabbed my forearms, and she said this five-to-ten-second prayer: *"Lord breaks down these walls."*

The Holy Spirit immediately entered me and freed me from every conceivable stronghold, both hidden and obvious, including my addiction to pornography as well as other vices like despair, anxiety, a distorted mind, the devil's lies, etc. My body felt as though it were being emptied out by a water bucket on the inside as I sensed the wind of God rushing down. It seems as though God gave me life, and He performed a supernatural act. I've been on fire for the Lord ever since He set me free, and I've never wanted to lead a mediocre Christian life.

I transitioned from being a follower of Jesus to a believer. My life had been changed by the Lord, and I yearned for Him above all else. So, with good intentions, I disciplined myself in the Scriptures. I am a teacher/pastor in the fivefold call of the Lord; without Him, I would not be the person I am today. Let me give you an update on my IQ level. I've increased my IQ from a range of 75 to 79 in August 2023 to around an IQ of 123. It's not to brag about how brilliant I am, but rather how God's glory has been made visible in my life, causing me to become the person I am today as a result of Christ.

And how I grew as a Christian was by trusting the Lord and allowing Him to run my life. I went from being addicted to my bad habits to working on my habits, such as reading books. I hate reading books, but God's grace allowed me to discipline myself into doing hard things, even if I didn't feel like it. Nowadays, we see that people look for a *'feeling' rather* than a doing. However, love is birthed from truth.

Discovering True Healing and Purpose in God's Love

Some of you reading this feel this way. *"How can I change God's opinion of me or become healed? How can a man named Jesus heal my illnesses the way He healed mine? He doing that seems to be beyond His power."* You see, I had made an effort to mend relationships using my own resources, to repent of my faults, and to work toward receiving Him. He can help and heal you with whatever you're going through, I want to assure you. For you to experience full freedom, He finished it on the Cross.

As the body, we must become humble and recognize in our hearts that we require not only a Savior but also that Jesus Christ be made Lord of our lives. He can do way more than we can imagine (see Ephesians 3:20), not just give you a place in heaven, because eternal life begins the moment you become a Christian. It's about bringing heaven into us, not about getting there. What purpose does life serve if we realize that we are not creating a new life with Him? Our calling is to follow Jesus, not to follow worldly callings. If the Gospel is not the entire message, the Church is missing something. We consider more of ourselves than His death on the Cross. It's also His burial and resurrection, for which there is a revelation and a reason why it is powerful in what Jesus did. The Gospel is restoring the relationship with the Father. Sin separates us from the Father, not the Father separating Himself from us.

Think about this: Why look for a source from the world that tries to fill the void in our hearts, knowing that it isn't enough for us to be satisfied? I am speaking on the terms of idolatry or even putting Him aside for something else. Even the Preacher in the book of Ecclesiastes had everything in the world but was never satisfied with anything but God. To fear Him and keep His commandments. Many in the body of Christ, I believe, turn away from the revelation of the Cross due to a lack of acknowledgment of who He truly is according to the Word. Some look at sources such as alcohol, pornography, drugs, and worldly relationships to find satisfaction and even materialistic things. What's worse is not seeing the presence of God due to unbelief. That is why discipleship is so important, because it creates an emphasis on building born-again believers into pointing and leading them to Jesus.

We don't just accept Him and figure out what we do for ourselves afterward. Jesus gave up His life so we could receive life. We were born with life in Him, not just His death. In later chapters, I will discuss how we bear eternal fruit. Not the fruit we receive from Him that has an expiration date you see in stores and only keeps us for a season. The lasting fruit is eternal and shapes our view of God and ourselves. Fruit that doesn't come from working towards but from simply abide in Him. And so when Jesus came, many were clueless that the Messiah had come to the world and fulfilled all the works of God according to the Word.

This book isn't a self-improving discipline book, but it promotes the lifestyle that I believe is what God would want us to do in our lives. Most importantly, having friendship with the Lord is more significant than settling for the title of man or woman of God. Life becomes easier when we follow Jesus through the toughest battles, yet He gives us rest and makes life easier because of His yoke (see Matthew 11:28–30). I am not speaking of a defeated view—that we allow sin to reign because the enemy tempts us, then we get worried, and then we trip and fall down the stairs. Or we kind of *"repent"* from porn and then return to it the next night. Fear is what drives people to remain or become indecisive. Sin is horrific and evil. In Christ, we are washed, clean, unleavened, and righteous because of His blood. The power of sin is destroyed for those who come to Him.

The Word of God, I believe, contains a lot of past-tense stuff that we have now in Christ. Jesus said, *"It is finished!"* If He says that, then the power of sin won't reign in our lives because He took sin upon Himself, including sickness, death, fears, temptations [1], strongholds, etc. Then, we follow Him and walk on the path of life. Let's look at an example of a passage in Ephesians in which Paul talks about our Christian Walk:

"So this I say and affirm together with the Lord, that you walk no longer just as the Gentiles also walk, in the futility of their mind, being darkened in their understanding, excluded from the life of God because of the ignorance that is in them, because of the hardness of their heart; and they, having become callous, have given themselves over to sensuality for the practice of every kind of impurity with greediness. But you did not learn Christ in this way, if indeed you have heard Him and have been taught in Him, just as truth is in Jesus, that, in reference to your former manner of life, you lay aside the old self, which is being corrupted in accordance with the lusts of deceit, and that you be renewed in the spirit of your mind, and put on the new self, which in the likeness of God has been created in righteousness and holiness of the truth." (Ephesians 4:7-24)

Take a moment and think, *"What am I believing that contradicts the truth?"* A lie contradicts the truth, but deception is believing in the lie. Jesus is the Son the Father has given us to be with so that we can inherit His glory by sacrificing Himself on the Cross. You see, God has always wanted us from the start. He created Adam so He could have a relationship with him. God's most prominent design was intimacy.

A relationship with God isn't something you have to perform or work for. It's a covenant relationship you have made after you said *"Yes"* to Him. He sought to have a relationship with His creation, which is humanity. Even before the foundations of the world, the Father, the Son, and the Holy Spirit worked together in a relationship. It's all part of the unit, yet they are One. An example is: if you're a mother or father, would you want the best for your children? Would you like to help your children grow more in Christ?

Would you want to encourage your kids to develop into people who can advance His kingdom while enhancing the world? Consider this: if you are a parent right now, or if you hope to be one day, you would plan or consider what would be best for your children. Remember that raising your children is not something you decide to do. God wants to provide you with wisdom so that you can raise your children. What is God's will, you ask? His Word speaks life and truth; we ask Him for the wisdom behind our actions. It is faith that produces good works. We come before Him confidently to the throne room to receive His power and grace to be more like Him and to treat our kids, neighbors, and spouses the way *He sees it*. The way we love our neighbor is the way *He loves them*.

Restoring Relationships and Connecting with God

Apostle Paul said, *"Intimate me as I intimidate Christ"* (see 1 Corinthians 11:1). It's simpler than we think. If we want His grace, we must come low and humble before Him. We must recognize that we cannot give our best to our relationships with one another based on our strengths or self-righteousness. We cannot use our natural, earthly, or even demonic wisdom and understanding to solve the issues in our lives (see James 3:13–18). I am mainly talking about this point in relationships. Every one of us in our lives has had a broken relationship with someone. The first ever broken relationship was with God with Adam and Eve. Sin is the root cause. Sin is a separation from Him. Before the fall, His relationship with Adam was so perfect that there was not a single ounce of separation between the two. It was perfect.

In marriage, a covenant is established between a man and a woman. The enemy's goal is to strategically cause separation and division in the marriage. Statistics say that forty to fifty percent of marriages end in divorce in the U.S. every year due to the root of sin or a prolonging of unrepentance. There are some issues in marriage that people face when it comes to money, reputation, work, et cetera. The Bible says the only right time to divorce someone is if their spouse commits sexual immortality (see Matthew 5:32). Anything else is considered outside the reason, and divorcing someone is considered adultery. There are billions of ways people divorce, and it is not God's design for men and women to separate. A relationship with God is the most important thing you want, especially before marriage. When God rules your marriage, there is no way the enemy can cause you to separate.

Another example is that we shouldn't be coming to other people about how we should approach God amid troubles and being reliant on the people, but instead, ask Him questions in our need by His will.

He is a good Father; He wants to watch over His children. As we open ourselves, He becomes more open to us. I don't deny the unity in the body; I fully support people bringing things to light, and it's biblical. However, there are cases where people have forgotten God's goodness, so if they went to someone for help, maybe they would hear them. It's about faith in God rather than faith in man.

The Good News is that God hears your heart. As we recognize that we need Him more than to save ourselves, we stay connected to the Father. In Matthew's book, a lawyer approached Jesus, asking Him what the great commandment was.

Jesus says, *"'You shall love the Lord your God with all your heart, and with all your soul, and with all your mind.' This is the great and foremost commandment. The second is like it: 'You shall love your neighbor as yourself.' On these two commandments depend the whole law and the prophets."* (Matthew 27:37-40).

You realize that the second comes after the first commandment. We love God with everything we have. We pour everything out to God. Every bit of us—our heart, soul, and mind. We become more reliant on the Lord, to the point that we act more like Him daily. It's not a figure of speech or a special phrase, but it's literal. Why? He's a God who is compassionate, gracious, slow to anger, and abounding in lovingkindness and truth.

"Whoever confesses that Jesus is the Son of God, God abides in him, and he in God. We have come to know and have believed

in the love that God has for us. God is love, and the one who abides in love abides in God, and God abides in him. By this, love is perfected with us, so that we may have confidence in the day of judgment; because as He is, so are we in this world. There is no fear in love, but perfect love casts out fear because fear involves punishment, and the one who fears is not perfected in love. We love because He first loved us." (1 John 4:15–19)

To stay intimate with the Lord as we remain consistent and faithful. It's like going to the gym. You know that to grow healthy and strong, you must be consistent, and you will start to notice the process. Considering even the pain that comes with all the workouts and the soreness, your body becomes more robust. Christianity is hard to follow; it is not easy, but life gets better with Him every day. Walking in spiritual discipline is essential, but not in a place of work or religion. We die for ourselves every day, and trials will come. Our faithfulness is being tested.

The good news is that James 1 says this: *"Consider it all joy, my brethren, when you encounter various trials, knowing that the testing of your faith produces endurance. And let endurance have its perfect result so that you may be perfect and complete, lacking in nothing." (James 1:2-4)*

Why? We know that Jesus is the perfect example of humanity by looking at the finished work of the Cross. It is vanity not to follow Him, but life gets simpler when we follow Him despite the troubles that come. We sit down at His feet, knowing He is faithful to us. He saw the joy ahead of Him (see Hebrews 12:2).

Now, I want to conclude this chapter with biblical evidence of how Jesus is the son of God. *John 3:16–17 ESV exclaims:*

"For God so loved the world that he gave his only Son, that whoever believes in him should not perish but have eternal life. For God did not send his Son into the world to condemn the world, but in order that the world might be saved through him."

Chapter 2: Awareness of our Walk

The Dangers of Hypocrisy and Missed Revelations

How *aware* are you of your walk with Him?

Are you aware of His precious presence?

What are the areas in which you can *judge* yourself righteously?

Jesus said to take the log out of your eye before taking the speck out of your brother's eye (see Matthew 7:1–5). The judge will be measured based on how you judge. To make a point, people may walk with God, know so much about scripture, and can't consider their issues. Consciously, it is easy to point yourself out; you may notice how you behave throughout the day, your thoughts, and even some sins you struggle with.

Deep within, you might unwittingly shield yourself from acknowledging your struggles, perhaps by focusing on others who grapple with similar shortcomings. It's a form of hypocrisy, a subtle deception we must guard against. Allow me to share this truth: those who have been reborn in faith are no longer identified as sinners; we are now recognized as righteous sons and daughters, saints of the Gospel (as articulated in 2 Corinthians 5:17; Romans 8:14–17; 1 Corinthians 6:11; Ephesians 2:19; 1 John 3:1–2).

In 2 Corinthians 5:17, we are reminded, "Therefore, if anyone is in Christ, the new creation has come: the old has gone, the new is here!" This verse emphasizes the transformative power of faith, turning us into new beings, free from the shackles of our former selves.

Romans 8:14–17 further affirms our elevated status, stating, *"For all who are being led by the Spirit of God, these are sons of God. For you have not received a spirit of slavery leading to fear again, but you have received a spirit of adoption as sons, by which we cry out, "Abba! Father!" The Spirit Himself testifies with our spirit that we are children of God, and if children, heirs also, heirs of God and fellow heirs with Christ, if indeed we suffer with Him so that we may also be glorified with Him."*

Here, we are assured of our divine heritage as children of God, co-heirs with Christ Himself. Furthermore, 1 Corinthians 6:11 echoes this transformation, declaring, *"But you were washed, sanctified, and justified in the name of the Lord Jesus Christ and by the Spirit of our God."* This verse emphasizes the purifying effect of faith, marking us as righteous and sanctified through the name of Jesus.

Ephesians 2:19 reinforces our new identity within the body of Christ: *"Consequently, you are no longer foreigners and strangers, but fellow citizens with God's people and also members of his household."* Through faith, we are adopted into God's family and welcomed as citizens of His divine kingdom.

Lastly, 1 John 3:1-2 beautifully encapsulates our exalted status: *"See what great love the Father has lavished on us, that we should be called children of God! And that is what we are! The world does not know us because it did not know him. Dear friends, now we are children of God, and what we will be has not yet been made known. But we know that when Christ appears, we shall be like him, for we shall see him as he is."* This passage illuminates the profound love the Father has bestowed upon us, affirming our identity as His cherished children, destined to share in the likeness of Christ.

So, my friend, let this truth resonate within you: you are no longer bound by the label of a sinner, but rather, you stand as a righteous, redeemed child of God, an heir to His eternal glory. Embrace this identity and live with the freedom it brings.

Many may know so much doctrine, theology, and culture and still struggle with pride, jealousy, comparison, et cetera. Consider the Pharisees during Jesus' time. The Pharisees were the most influential religious group within Judaism. A religious group you can truly rely on when looking at scripture. They have been highly resourceful, with countless recorded documents passed down from Genesis to Malachi. By age seven, many Pharisees had already memorized the Torah.

Most Pharisees opposed Jesus, pointing out the 'heresy' Jesus was preaching. They were self-righteous, hypocritical, and unaware of the picture God was showing. Jesus said: "They do not practice what they preach" (see Matthew 23:3) because they have the correct views on God, the Father, but missed out that Jesus is the same God that came down from Heaven in the flesh. The same God they studied, worshipped, and prayed to, yet can't see the truth. They were so close to seeing the revelation of who Jesus was. Nicodemus was one of the few who believed Jesus was a Teacher from God.

Considering the miracles Jesus performed and the way He preached, it influenced the idea that Nicodemus saw Him as the Messiah to come. The Pharisees have waited for so many years for a Messiah to come, yet they didn't catch on to what the picture was. God created this picture of Jesus, the image of the invisible God. To show humanity that the Messiah is already in the flesh. Heaven was silent when Jesus arrived. The Pharisees encountered Jesus many times in public but didn't encounter the revelation of the Father's Son. They missed the mark.

Even more astonishing is that both the Pharisees and the Romans bore witness to His divine presence. After Jesus' resurrection, the Roman guards stationed at the tomb awoke to a miraculous sight. They hurriedly reported this extraordinary event to Caiaphas, the high priest. In a desperate attempt to conceal the truth, Caiaphas resorted to bribery, compelling the guards to spread a fabricated account—one that alleged the disciples had stolen Jesus' body, as recounted in Matthew 28:11–15. It's a perplexing turn of events, isn't it?

Matthew 28:11–15 reads, *"As the women were on their way, some of the guards went into the city and told the leading priests what had happened. A meeting with the elders was called, and they decided to give the soldiers a large bribe. They told the soldiers, "You must say, 'Jesus' disciples came during the night while we were sleeping, and they stole his body.' If the governor hears about it, we'll stand up for you so you won't get in trouble." So the guards accepted the bribe and said what they were told to say. Their story spread widely among the Jews, and they still tell it today."*

This passage underscores the lengths some were willing to go to suppress the extraordinary truth of Jesus' resurrection. The collision between religious leaders and Roman guards serves as a reminder of the powerful impact that Christ's resurrection had on those who witnessed it firsthand. The

Roman guards encountered His presence and acknowledged it was the power of the Lord. It was the lusts of their flesh that satisfied them more. The money satisfied their hearts more than God had offered because the natural, visible realm has more to offer. It's the lustful desire to take what is theirs and leave off the importance of the manifestation power of God.

"For the love of money is a root of all sorts of evil, and some, by longing for it, have wandered away from the faith and pierced themselves with many griefs." (1 Timothy 6:10)

There's nothing wrong with money, but it's about what you love more. Walking in God's desires is crucial because it fulfills our purpose, brings God's blessings into our lives, strengthens our relationship with Him, allows us to influence others positively, and contributes to a better world. Take note of this and see what areas of your life God can help you grow in.

We discover our purpose and direction when we align our lives with God's desires. We experience His favor, grow closer to Him, inspire those around us, and promote justice and love. Living this way enables us to lead a purposeful, blessed, connected, and impactful life. We reflect God's character and bring glory to Him.

Surrendering to God's Plan and Embracing His Greater Promises

Now think about this: What is something that satisfies our flesh? Galatians 5:17 says, "For the flesh sets its desire against the Spirit, and the Spirit against the flesh; for these are in opposition to one another, so that you may not do the things that you please."

The difference between the unrepented Roman soldier and the believer in the flesh is that the Romans willingly went for the money without conviction of the Holy Spirit. When we have the Holy Spirit, the Spirit convicts us of our sins. Conviction simply means to be convinced to do better according to His will.

Instead of relying solely on our abilities, we depend on the Holy Spirit to guide us and empower us in every aspect of our lives, even when we may not feel connected to Him.

Being aware of the Holy Spirit's presence and working in our lives means aligning ourselves with His perspective and recognizing Him for who He truly is. He is a person who doesn't want to be grieved. Despite the circumstances that we have experienced, the Holy Spirit can lead people to encounter God's truth through the Scriptures, interactions with others, and His divine knowledge.

Receiving the Holy Spirit's guidance is as simple as accepting a gift, yet many people struggle to trust Him fully. The reasons for this hesitation may vary, but it is an important question.

Most people are afraid to give themselves up to the Lord. People are scared to give up their old lives because there's something good behind their lifestyle. I remember seeing an illustration online of a little girl holding a normal-sized teddy bear.

Standing in front of her was Jesus. Jesus told her to give the teddy bear to Him, but behind Him was a giant teddy bear prepared for the little girl. However, the little girl was afraid to give up her current one because she loved the teddy bear, yet she was unaware of something greater ahead. Everyone has something dear to us that fills our satisfaction, but God has something far greater than we can imagine.

The sacred scriptures reprimand us to relinquish our desires, shoulder the weight of our crosses, and walk in the footsteps of Christ. Often, we find ourselves tightly clinging to our earthly treasures, our spouses, our families, and the reputation we've built over time. These attachments, though meaningful, can sometimes become stumbling blocks on our spiritual journey.

It makes sense to acknowledge that a lot of people have trouble believing. This lack of faith frequently makes it difficult for people to recognize and accept God's goodness, mainly when influenced by the theological lessons they were nurtured with. Preconceived conceptions and deeply held ideas might obscure our perception of the divine, making it difficult to completely appreciate the breadth of God's kindness and love.

However, we find the greatest freedom and intimacy with the Holy Spirit in severing these earthly bonds and tearing down the walls of skepticism. We become more aware of God's limitless grace when we let go of our attachments and submit to the Holy Spirit. We are able to more fully live out the teachings of Christ by sacrificing ourselves for the sake of a greater good because of this life-changing act of faith.

In this self-denial and spiritual growth process, we find a sense of liberation. The burdens we once carried are lightened, and we discover an abiding peace that exceeds the temporal. As we begin and go through our spiritual journey, we realize that our greatest wealth is not in material possessions but in our relationship with our Creator and our ability to show love and kindness to others.

Through the grace of God, we are granted the capacity to see beyond the confines of our understanding and to embrace a fuller, richer experience of His boundless goodness and love.

There is nothing more remarkable than our Lord, Jesus Christ. The Son of Man, who takes away the sin of the world! (see John 1:29) Christ came so we could be free from the power of sin.

Giving up things that we hold dear can be an arduous task. I remember how challenging it was to let go of the things I enjoyed. During my growing-up years, I was highly addicted to video games, starting with my Nintendo 3DS and moving on to my custom PC gaming desktop. I even aspired to become a computer scientist after high school.

The amount that technology has advanced since the turn of the twenty-first century shocked me. Until I realized how dependent *I was* on Him, I wanted to do everything on my own. I was able to see God's goodness and remove the veil that had been blinding me by setting aside the things I cherished.

Nothing held greater significance than the blood of the lamb. May the Lamb that was slain receive the reward of His suffering.

Embracing Our Identity as Children of God and Living with Kingdom Purpose

Before Christ, I was overcome by dread and stuck in sin, but the Lord brought me out of it. Accepting Him was easy, even though He seemed too good to be true. I was raised with half my life devoted to Jesus and half to the world. Like the Roman soldier, I was unaware of God's potential, even though I felt His presence. The knowledge that would ultimately free me from sin's grip was hidden because of my ignorance. Our culture shapes who we are and how we live. Certain body members impact us in some way, regardless of whether we are raised as Pentecostals, Presbyterians, Baptists, or Anabaptists. We are impacted by either God or the world in every part of our lives.

Our upbringing and how we view God and other people shape our minds. Our innate talents, qualities, and traits have been passed down through the generations since Adam's creation. God distributes people's gifts to themselves rather than using them to create the body. Consider the most brilliant people on earth who are well-known all over the world yet live unethical lives.

How absurd, yet I wonder: what would happen if everyone used their gifts to further the kingdom of God? I consider myself fortunate to see preachers preaching to people worldwide to help them reconcile with God in public spaces and in other countries. Many people are lost due to sin; some are even deceived by doctrine that does not lead to life.

My heart burns for people to know who Christ is. Even those who are saved yet lack truth are people who live an orphan lifestyle that tries to please God when God is pleased with His children according to faith. Theology is the principle that influences our lives.

Once again, the book of Romans says we have received the spirit of adoption as sons. Romans says: *"For all who the Spirit of God is leading, these are sons of God. For you have not received a spirit of slavery leading to fear again, but you have received a spirit of adoption as sons, by which we cry out, "Abba! Father!" The Spirit Himself testifies with our spirit that we are children of God, and if children, heirs also, heirs of God and fellow heirs with Christ, if indeed we suffer with Him so that we may also be glorified with Him" (Romans 8:14–17).*

Embracing Rest and Surrender in Our Relationship with God

Suppose we struggle to believe we aren't near Him. We would see Him as a Master. He is our Master, but that's not just who He is. He is our Father in Heaven who is relational. I have seen men of God who felt so condemned and worked hard to receive His affection. However, the book of Romans says there is no condemnation in Christ Jesus (see Romans 8:1). I have also seen people struggle with the Law (which is the law that the Israelites depended on in the old covenant) and never want to do anything with sin. Yet they sin because they know the Law and not Him. I believe the most significant struggle most Christians face is the Law because it's something we have to behold and look at to keep us upright. A believer knows that watching pornography is a sin, but being more conscious of the Law is what causes us to stumble due to the Law. The goal of the Christian life is not to fulfill the laws, it's to follow Jesus who has already fulfilled them for us, and in that we will fulfill the Law. God has given us Laws to stay right with Him. There's nothing wrong with the Law, but people live under the Law and not the power of His grace. It's about beholding the King who's done it all.

Jesus makes it clear in His deep teachings that His goal was to bring the Law and the Prophets to their complete meaning and fulfillment, not to do away with them (Matthew 5:17). Through our unshakeable faith in His completed work on the cross, He offers us a route to ultimate freedom. His life and self-sacrificing death were the pinnacles of divine creation.

Matthew 5:17 reads, *"Do not think that I have come to abolish the Law or the Prophets; I have not come to abolish them but to fulfill them."* These words serve as a cornerstone of Christ's ministry, affirming the continuity and fulfillment of the Old Testament scriptures through His life, death, and resurrection.

Therefore, an eternal pursuit of the finished work of the cross is a sign of mature faith. It is a daily effort, a purposeful pursuit of Christ, to get to know Him more deeply. This endeavor originates from a position of rest and faith in His grace rather than from striving or effort.

We understand that true spiritual development in this endeavor does not imply a final destination or a state of perfection. Rather, it is characterized by a modest recognition that we are still learning and developing in our relationship with Christ. It's an attitude that acknowledges our continual need for Him, our reliance on His grace, and our unwavering trust in His transformative power.

So, let us strive for maturity, not as a final destination, but as a lifelong commitment to seeking Christ and embracing the profound depth of His finished work on the cross. Through this, we discover a freedom that transcends earthly constraints and a relationship with our Savior that is boundless and everlasting.

The book of Hebrews says, *"Let us press on to maturity and leave from the elementary teaching about Christ." (Hebrews 6:1)* Of course, learning the foundation of Christ means never laying down a foundation of repentance of dead works and faith toward God. We must believe what He has done to us. Please do not stop yourself from knowing Him more.

There's so much more to knowing Him than what you think. We have to repent of that idea of being satisfied and avoid growth. God seeks us every millisecond of our lives. We may not see it, we may not feel it, and we may not hear it, but He is present. He wants to be invited. He is there for us in our lives, in the highest or lowest parts. He is our source for everything. We cannot underestimate His power to transform our lives into becoming more like Him.

Surrender is one of the aspects of intimacy with Him, but knowing rest is what gives us His grace and favor. We humble ourselves before Him so we can inherit His glory—the glory of standing right with God. The Holy Spirit is what helps us stay close. Jesus is our meditator. When we pray to the Father, the

Son comes first. Jesus says many times in scripture that we can only access the Father through the Son. And so, how important is it for us to seek Him? It's beyond our comprehension.

"5 Or do you think that the Scripture speaks to no purpose: "He jealously desires the Spirit which He has made to dwell in us"? 6 But He gives a greater grace. Therefore, it says, "God is opposed to the proud but gives grace to the humble." 7 Submit therefore to God. Resist the devil, and he will flee from you. 8 Draw near to God, and He will draw near to you. Cleanse your hands, you sinners, and purify your hearts, you double-minded. (James 4:5-8)

In the depths of time, even before we took our first breaths in our mother's womb, God desired and knew us intimately (as affirmed in Jeremiah 1:5). Such is His boundless love for us that He made the ultimate sacrifice, sending His precious Son to lay down His life for our sake.

Jeremiah 1:5 reminds us, *"Before I formed you in the womb, I knew you; before you were born, I set you apart; I appointed you as a prophet to the nations."* This verse encapsulates God's profound, preordained purpose for each of us, underscoring the depths of His love and intentionality.

If you find yourself burdened, weighed down by the cares and troubles of life, know this: God stands ready to lift that weight from your shoulders, replacing it with a peace that surpasses all understanding. As Jesus Himself declared in Matthew 11:28–30, *"Come to me, all you who are weary and burdened, and I will give you rest. Take my yoke upon you and learn from me, for I am gentle and humble in heart, and you will find rest for your souls. For my yoke is easy, and my burden is light."* This promise serves as a beacon of hope, offering peace and respite to all who turn to Him.

The beauty lies in its simplicity. Much like reclining on a couch after a long day, finding rest in Christ is a gesture of trust and surrender. It requires no grand effort or elaborate ritual. It is an invitation to lean back into the loving embrace of our Savior, allowing Him to bear our burdens and provide the peace that only He can offer.

So, if you find yourself burdened and restless, remember these promises and the truth. Know that God has known you and loved you from the very beginning. Love is a choice, and He chose to love you before He anything else and wanted you to be on Earth. He longs to grant you a peace that transcends all understanding. With open arms, He beckons you to come, find rest, and experience the profound lightness of His yoke.

"We love, because He first loved us." (1 John 4:19)

The Costly Worship of Surrendering Our Most Precious Offerings

In the same way, you can sit with the Lord as quickly as that. Unbelief is the most extensive wall we have to keep breaking down daily. The more we break our alabaster jars before Him, the more we become free. The sign of worship is giving up ourselves as a living sacrifice (see Romans 12:2).

One of my favorite Gospel stories is about Mary and the alabaster jar when she breaks the jar before Jesus and spills her hair onto his feet. The disciples chastised Mary for not passing one of the most costly jars ever. The Bible states that the cost exceeds a year's salary.

John Piper claims in an article that the approximate value of an eleven-ounce flask of nard was $25,000. [1] That's how much a 2020 Volkswagen Passat is in the present time! She sacrificed one of her finest pieces in the act of worship. Jesus told His disciples that what she did was not in vain and said Mary would be remembered when people preach the Gospel (see Matthew 26:13).

Mary sought intimacy with Him with all her heart. God designed intimacy by showing His love and affection toward us by showing Adam in the communion of the Holy Spirit and then to Eve when she came. Adam needed to have a physical being to show his love to his wife, Eve, with his natural eyes. I believe that for infants or children of the faith, it is easier to believe in Him because there isn't a physical being that's presented in front of them. Children believe in almost anything, but it's revealing the reality that there is a living God who cares for His children.

Encountering His Presence and the Transformative Power of Belief

We need proof in order to believe. To make a statement in court, a judge must consider the evidence presented by both sides. For us to see His splendor, Jesus sent the Holy Spirit. Though He is invisible to us, we may sense Him approaching us like a wind. He will always be present for those who encounter Him for the first time. Even though we don't feel it after being born again and filled with the Holy Spirit, God is still at work. A genuine contact with the Holy Spirit is what constitutes a sincere experience of being born-again. If you ask, the Holy Spirit is always willing to meet with you.

No matter how our walk looks with the Lord, we can praise the Highest One because He finished the work for us on the cross by taking our record and replacing it with His perfect record. He is perfect; there isn't a single mark off in His record— a straight-A student of God. The only issue I don't want people to have regarding doctrine is not taking action to walk out like Him. I don't want to see people feeling down and saying, *"I praise God still at the end,"* with a defeated view. As Christians, we don't diminish our emotions, however, it's important to recognize what we can do to prevent a false mindset of who God is. An example of scripture is in Philippians:

"Do all things without grumbling or disputing; so that you will prove yourselves to be blameless and innocent, children of God above reproach in the midst of a crooked and perverse generation, among whom you appear as lights in the world, holding fast the word of life, so that in the day of Christ I will have reason to glory because I did not run in vain nor toil in vain." (Philippians 2:14-16)

It's great that you praise Him, but do you believe what He's done in your life? Where is your heart? I would much rather see people transformed by His fruits than see people stuck in their lifestyle and say they praise Him without action or belief.

It's an orphan mindset to be in. Recognize that you are a child of God who is blameless and innocent.

The religious act that we need to measure ourselves to be right with God is to be pleased by Him when He is already pleased with us in that we can now have deep intimacy with Him. I have seen people who share their testimonies weekly in youth services who feel so down about what they have been doing lately and say, *"I praise God still."* Where's the fruit behind that and the confidence? It's one thing that there's a lack of intimacy, but it's another thing that we know there's a God who loved us and made us clean and right. Sadness isn't a fruit. That's a lie of the enemy when we should be receiving the fruit of joy instead. The nine fruits of the spirit in Galatians say,

"But the fruit of the Spirit is love, joy, peace, patience, kindness, goodness, faithfulness, gentleness, and self-control; against such things, there is no law" (Galatians 5:22–23). If you aren't experiencing any of these fruits, something's wrong. What is the one thing you lack? He gives us all of these fruits. We must see that our heavenly Father is more significant than our circumstances and troubles. What's terrible about sin is that it becomes normalized for most. It's a dangerous mindset. Our encounters are what shape our beliefs.

Our thoughts, emotions, decisions, and behavior come from our beliefs. Behavior is the outcome of our encounters. It's self-explanatory; however, we aren't consciously aware of how encounters affect our lives in the same way pornography affects many lives worldwide. Sometimes, it's obvious to spot, but sometimes it deteriorates without repentance. Whether one encounter is good or bad—one encounter, one decision—determines how we grow out of it. That's why it is so important to watch our hearts.

Scripture isn't about understanding what goes on in the Word but about the application that changes and transforms our lives. The only issue is that our flesh craves something sinful. Yet it's the reason Christ came to destroy the power of sin in that we don't have to be reigned by our fleshly desires.

To receive His Spirit into our spirit-man.

2 Corinthians says: *"Therefore, if anyone is in Christ, he is a new creature; the old things passed away; behold, new things have come. Now all these things are from God, who reconciled us to Himself through Christ and gave us the ministry of reconciliation." (2 Corinthians 5:17–18).*

If you believe you were made new, you are a new creature. You are no longer part of this world, yet you're being set apart from the earth through reconciliation. As Isaiah 11:2 says, we become more like Him through the spirit of counsel through which He leads us to the right path. We start to begin the process of sanctification once we're born again. The more we separate ourselves from the world with the help of the Holy Spirit, the more we become like Him. We're also justified in getting rid of the penalty of sin by His grace. Romans says, *"For all have sinned and fall short of the glory of God, being justified as a gift by His grace through the redemption which is in Christ Jesus" (Romans 3:23–24).*

The Simplicity and Distortion of the Gospel

We all have sinned, but by the riches of His mercy, we are reconciled back to the Father. It's good news, seriously. The Gospel is so simple. We have to go to the basics of the Gospel.

There is no other Gospel than what the Bible says. The Gospel is the death, burial, and resurrection of Jesus Christ, but most importantly, the relationship with the Father. He was crucified, so we can be crucified with Him (see Galatians 2:20). He was buried, so we are buried with Him (see Colossians 3:3). And we're resurrected with Him (see Romans 6:5).

Why are people not being transformed by this when they have known Christ for a long time? It's unbelief. I will keep mentioning the word 'unbelief' because people underestimate how God can move in their lives more than they think of Him by the power of the Holy Spirit. God isn't mad at your sins. He isn't angry that you backslide and believe in a lie that you wouldn't think He would consider you worthy of His time.

He wants to restore the things that are broken.

I've encountered folks who strayed from their religion. Either the world is attacking them or the Church is injuring them. Perhaps since some people desire worldly goods, the Church experience or theology they were raised with didn't make sense to them and insulted them. Maybe their hearts were affected by sin, and they left the Church because they *"felt"* they didn't need it.

Possibly, many looked at the Gospel the wrong way, and the Church is missing out on what the Gospel is. The presentation of the Gospel is misused. You may have heard or seen the hate, love, and versions of the Gospels created by man's understanding. Each one is focused on one idea of the Gospel but used incorrectly, and some are heretical. The Apostle Paul wrote a letter to Galatia, and in the first chapter of Galatians, he says this:

*"I am amazed that you are so quickly deserting Him who called you by the grace of Christ, for a different gospel; **7** which is really not another; only there are some who are disturbing you and want to distort the gospel of Christ. But even if we, or an angel from heaven, should preach to you a gospel contrary to what we have preached to you, he is to be accursed! As we have said before, so I say again now, if any man is preaching to you a gospel contrary to what you received, he is to be arrested! Am I now seeking the favor of men, or of God? Or am I striving to please men? If I were still trying to please men, I would not be a bond servant of Christ. For I would have you know, brethren, that the gospel that was preached by me is not according to man. For I neither received it from man, nor was I taught it, but I received it through a revelation of Jesus Christ." (Galatians 1:6-12)*

Paul is agitated because people are turning away from the straightforward gospel truth. Paul declares that he will punish anyone spreading a different gospel than he preached. It draws people away from the only reality. Keep an open mind and use your discernment to weigh God's word against what you see or hear. Seek the insight and knowledge of the Lord. Keep your theology in check if it lacks evidence of intimacy.

It's challenging to convince someone of their personal beliefs (regarding those outside of Christianity) because of the influence of culture, religion, false spirits, et cetera. It takes a lot of sacrifice and humility to change someone's view. When preaching the Gospel to an unbeliever, many will feel awkward.

They think, *"Why is this person telling me about Jesus?"* or even this, too: *"Why am I hearing this when I go to Church? That's all I need to be secure in my faith."*

Lukewarmness is simply, in one view, living in the world of sin while going to Church.

I firmly believe it's even more dangerous when someone says to themselves they go to Church with a negative attitude or seem to care less. You may understand what I mean if you ever evangelized someone. You can get someone's attention, but once Jesus is involved, people turn away or ignore the message that can transform their lives. You can also see them by their fruit and the way they respond. Someone who can relate to us but is not truly interested in the relationship with God. It's a sign of lukewarmness.

The Bible says you can tell by their fruits (see Matthew 7:16–20). You can tell who is a good or bad tree because trees can't carry different fruit. Each tree has its own products, such as apple or orange trees. An orange tree cannot bear an apple. It's a simple seed that produces something spectacular in the eyes of God. In order to convince someone about Jesus, you must trust and fully rely on the Holy Spirit, because He is the greatest evangelist and He is the one who convicts their hearts to repentance.

Chapter 3: The Seed and the Law

The Seed and the Law: The Journey of Growth: From Seed to Fruitfulness

A seed must die in order to grow. Dying to believe that you would receive life from Him. When you're born again, there is a seed sown into your soul. Your life is flipped upside down, and you meet Jesus for the first time. There isn't a more significant experience than that. I could have started this chapter at the beginning of this book. It would make sense because this book is about intimacy and how the world around us influences us. This book is for anyone. I want to talk about this topic because I want to learn how believers can grow in Christ. It doesn't matter how old you are or if you just got born; whether you're a baby Christian or a mature son, it doesn't matter. We can grow even more remarkable than we think with Christ. We do have to repent if we believe our walk with Christ is as good as it is or should be. There are a lot of areas in our lives where we can grow. His grace is sufficient for us to grow, and we must abide by His grace.

"But the seed falling on good soil refers to someone who hears the word and understands it. This is the one who produces a crop, yielding a hundred, sixty, or thirty times what was sown."

The verse Matthew 13:23 uses the analogy of a seed being planted in the soil to explain the potential for growth and fruitfulness in individuals who hear and understand the word.

The verse begins by stating that once planted in the ground, a seed has the potential to grow and bear fruit. In this analogy, the seed represents the words or teachings given to individuals. When someone receives and understands these teachings, it is likened to a seed sown on good soil.

The verse explains that the person who hears and understands the word is compared to good soil. Just as good soil provides a favorable environment for a seed to grow, this person's receptive heart and understanding create the conditions for the seed to take root and produce fruit in their life.

The fruitfulness of the seed is described in terms of different yields: thirty-fold, sixty-fold, and one hundred-fold. It suggests that the impact and growth resulting from the word can vary among individuals. Some may bear fruit that is thirty times the initial seed, others sixty times, and some even a hundred times.

Overall, this verse emphasizes the importance of hearing and understanding the Word. It highlights that when the Word is received with an open heart and comprehended, it has the potential to bring about growth, transformation, and fruitfulness in the lives of individuals with varying degrees of abundance.

A seed takes a while to grow into a product or fruit. Depending on what kind of tree it is, whether it's a dwarf or standard-size tree, it would take two to eight years to bear fruit. Similarly to the Bible's saying that we bear good fruit, we must recognize that we don't bear much fruit the moment we're born again. You receive His life and the likeness of His nature, and then you grow in Christ depending on how you tend the plant. A believer leads someone to Christ; they accept and receive Him as a gift. They instantly became righteous and justified, and now you're in the process of what the Bible calls sanctification. I first want to touch what is justified and righteous before Him. To simply look at what it means, Romans says:

"But now, apart from the Law, the righteousness of God has been manifested, being witnessed by the Law and the Prophets, even the righteousness of God through faith in Jesus Christ for all those who believe; for there is no distinction; for all have sinned and fall short of the glory of God, being justified as a gift by His grace through the redemption which is in Christ Jesus, whom God displayed publicly as a propitiation in His blood through faith. This was to demonstrate His righteousness because, in the forbearance of God, He passed over the sins previously committed; for the demonstration, I say, of His righteousness at present, so that He would be just and the justifier of the one who has faith in Jesus." (Romans 3:21-27)

Romans 3:21–27 is a significant passage from the Bible that explains the concept of righteousness in relation to God's grace and the role of faith in Jesus Christ.

The verse begins by stating that, apart from the Law (referring to the Jewish law), the righteousness of God has been revealed. This righteousness is witnessed by the Law and the Prophets, which means that the Old Testament scriptures bear testimony to God's righteousness.

The passage continues to explain that this righteousness of God is made available to all people through faith in Jesus Christ, regardless of any distinctions such as ethnicity or social status. It emphasizes that all individuals have sinned and fallen short of God's glory, highlighting the universality of human sinfulness.

Even so, the good news is that believers are justified as a gift through God's grace. This justification is made possible through the redemption found in Jesus Christ. Jesus, through His sacrificial death and shedding of His blood, serves as a propitiation, satisfying the righteous requirements of God's justice. Through faith in Jesus, believers receive forgiveness and reconciliation with God. The passage further explains that God's display of His righteousness through Jesus' sacrifice demonstrates His justice. In the past, God had shown forbearance by not immediately punishing sins. However, this display of righteousness through Jesus shows that God is both just and the justifier of those who have faith in Jesus. In other words, God remains just by not overlooking or dismissing sin, but at the same time, He offers justification to believers who trust in Jesus.

Overall, this passage from Romans emphasizes that righteousness before God is not achieved through strict adherence to the Law but through faith in Jesus Christ. It highlights the universal need for redemption due to human sinfulness and emphasizes the grace and forgiveness offered through Jesus' sacrifice. It also highlights the demonstration of God's righteousness and justice in the plan of salvation.

Embracing Grace: The Journey of Transformation

When we accept Christ, we're set apart from the Law. Now, what is the Law? The Law God established in the Old Testament that we would have to follow daily. The only issue is that it was difficult to fulfill, and we could never be righteous with Jesus. The good news is that Jesus has finished His work for us. We receive His grace, which empowers us to become more like Him. It's a simple gift.

Now, the grace given to us is a gift to us. Grace means we receive mercy for our mistakes and become more like Jesus. Mercy, for example, is when you get pulled over by an officer on a freeway for speeding. An officer can punish the driver with a ticket, arrest, and many more options they can choose from, or just let the transgressor go with a warning. Mercy is like when an officer enables you to go with a warning. However, grace is like in the same cop scenario: the officer gives you mercy but gives you a thousand bucks afterward.

In His Word, we must see that everything we do is according to His will and not ours. The Lord may bless us, but it's about being faithful to what He calls us to do. And so when it comes to seed, our roots in our old foundation start to change and grow more fruit, but it takes time. Sanctification means that we become more set apart from the world. The more we grow into God's calling, the more we get set apart. And as Christ is buried, we are the seed planted underneath Him; our seed grows like He got up from the grave. The difference is that we inherit His life instantly through acceptance, but why don't we become like Him?

Romans 3:23 states, *"For all have sinned and fall short of the glory of God."* This verse acknowledges the universal reality that every person, with their fleshly nature, is prone to sin and falls short of God's perfect standard.

The distinction between humanity and Jesus lies in humans possessing a fleshly nature that is susceptible to sin over time. Jesus, on the other hand, came into the world in the flesh but was full of the Holy Spirit and life. He was without sin and did not succumb to the sinful tendencies of human nature.

As humans, we are born into a fallen world, carrying within us a sinful nature that inclines us towards wrongdoing. Our flesh can weigh us down, making it challenging to resist temptation and live according to God's will. However, the verse brings attention to the ongoing transformative work of God in our lives. Depending on our individual circumstances and spiritual journey, God is actively working to remove the fleshly influences from our lives.

It is important to note that although we can discern between good and evil, our actions often contradict what we know to be right. Our minds recognize what is good and bad, yet we sometimes find ourselves doing the things we hate. This internal struggle highlights the ongoing battle between the desires of the flesh and the desires of the spirit. Apostle Paul struggled with this, and he wrote in Romans, saying:

"For we know that the Law is spiritual, but I am of flesh, sold into bondage to sin. For what I am doing, I do not understand, for I am not practicing what I would like to do, but I am doing the very thing I hate. But if I do the very thing I do not want to do, I agree with the Law, confessing that the Law is good. So now, no longer am I the one doing it, but sin dwells in me. For I know that nothing good dwells in me, that is, in my flesh; for the willing is present in me, but the doing of the good is not. For the good that I want, I do not do it, but I practice the very evil that I

do not want. But if I am doing the very thing I do not want, I am no longer the one doing it, but sin, which dwells in me." (Romans 7:14-20)

Abiding in Christ: The Key to Fruitfulness

Please don't get confused about what you have just read. Just because we sinned doesn't mean we should continue it. Sin separates us from God; instead, we're supposed to be separated from the world. Paul talks about how the Law is good, so we know what is evil to God. When you're born again, you have a new inner man, the spirit in us; the outer man is the flesh. It is the flesh that enjoys what we used to like before we knew God that isn't good towards God. Our old behaviors, our sinful patterns, etc. That is why we're growing more into being like Jesus when a seed is planted. The more we abide in Him, the more we become like Him. John wrote one of Jesus' teachings on what it is to be a tree.

"I am the true vine, and My Father is the vinedresser. He takes away every branch in Me that does not bear fruit, and every branch that bears fruit, He prunes it so that it may bear more fruit. You are already clean because of the Word I have spoken to you. Abide in Me, and I in you. As the branch cannot bear fruit of itself unless it abides in the vine, neither can you unless you abide in Me. I am the vine; you are the branches; he who abides in Me and I in him, he bears much fruit, for apart from Me you can do nothing. If anyone does not abide in Me, he is thrown away as a branch and dries up; they gather them, cast them into the fire, and burn them. If you abide in Me, and My words abide in you, ask whatever you wish, and it will be done for you. This glorifies my Father that you bear much fruit and so

prove to be My disciples. Just as the Father has loved Me, I have also loved you; abide in My love. If you keep My commandments, you will abide in My love, just as I have kept My Father's commandments and abided in His love. These things I have spoken to you so that My joy may be in you and that your joy may be made full." (John 15:1-11)

In this passage, Jesus refers to Himself as the true vine and God the Father as the vinedresser or gardener. He explains that the Father takes away every branch that is connected to Him but does not bear fruit. However, the Father pruned the branches that do bear fruit to encourage even greater fruitfulness.

Jesus then invites His disciples to abide in Him, emphasizing the importance of staying connected to Him just as a branch is connected to the vine. He highlights that, apart from Him, they can do nothing of lasting significance. Jesus uses the imagery of the vine and branches to illustrate believers' vital and dependent relationship with Him.

Continuing His teaching, Jesus emphasizes the importance of abiding in Him and having His Words abide in His followers. He assures them that if they remain in Him and His words remain in them, they can ask whatever they wish, and it will be done for them. It highlights the power of prayer and the alignment of desires with God's will that comes from abiding in Jesus.

Jesus further explains that by bearing much fruit, His followers bring glory to God the Father and demonstrate their discipleship. He stresses the importance of abiding in His love and keeping His commandments, just as He has kept His Father's commandments and abides in His love.

Lastly, Jesus shares these teachings so that His joy may be in His disciples and their joy may be complete. He desires His followers to experience the fullness of joy that comes from remaining connected to Him and living in obedience to His teaching.

The Process of Abiding: Surrender, Pruning, and Joyful Transformation

When we submit to Jesus daily, we bear the fruits of what Paul has been saying to Galatia. What is love, what is joy, and what is peace? And so forth. Christ came so that we could be with Him. Not next to us, around us, or above us, but inside of us as one flesh. I read this passage from John and saw how practical it seemed. But what does it look like to a new believer? What does it mean to abide? It is simply to believe first what He can do to your life and how to submit in humility. How does God work? What is the process? Apostle Paul said this:

"I planted, Apollos watered, but God was causing the growth. Neither the one who plants nor the one who waters is anything but God who causes the growth. Now, he who plants and waters is one, but each will receive his own reward according to his own labor. For we are God's fellow workers; you are God's field, God's building. (1 Corinthians 3:6–9)

God is the only person who causes growth. A man can help a person's development with the Holy Spirit, but God always causes things to grow secretly. Paul wanted the Corinth Church to see that it was not looking at him or Apollos but at God. You start to bear good fruit when you look at Him and only Him. It's acknowledging Him and going low before Him. We can grow fruit faster, or it may take longer. God prunes the rotten fruit out of the branches, which is us, and throws away the rotten fruit. And the more we seek Him, the more we grow more fruitful. Put it this way: you wouldn't even try to eat bad fruit. You would always want to choose to eat good fruit. It's part of our morality to determine what is good for us. In the same essence, why not seek what is good in our lives? It's common sense, but our human behavior or the flesh doesn't see the significance it can bring.

The flesh does whatever it wants; our behaviors determine how we approach God. The fear of man, for instance, shapes how we behave toward people—the fear of what people will think, how we approach our friends, and many more. I'm sure everyone has some kind of anxiety in their lives, but it can be sanctified and renewed with full assurance of peace. God prunes the fruit of anxiety when we abide in Him. When we seriously trust Him, He can do much good. It's not about what level you're giving Him. It's about going all in for Him. There will be suffering behind the pruning, but there's joy behind the suffering. The gospel is simple, but there's a reality of suffering that makes us more like Christ.

Beholding Christ: The Key to Transformation and Bearing Fruit

Consider Jesus: He was without fault yet willingly endured the cross to secure our freedom. According to Jewish custom, He endured thirty-nine lashes, each one containing a whip embedded with tiny fragments of glass. As the whip struck His body, the shards would penetrate the skin, causing it to tear and peel away when removed.

This physical ordeal serves as a metaphor for our own spiritual growth. Just as Jesus took upon Himself the burden of our sins, effectively putting to death our sinful nature, so too must we undergo a transformative process. Our old selves, represented by the flesh, must be stripped away, allowing us to inherit His divine life. This process commences with self-denial, surrendering our own desires, and embracing His will. We must firmly believe that our sinful nature was crucified alongside Jesus on the cross, forever eradicated.

Although this is a historical event, it is crucial to reflect on whether we still live as if it were the present. It is easy to claim that we have moved on, but if this claim is untrue, what meaningful change can we bring about? Imagine entering a crowded room carrying something deeply personal. Outward appearances may deceive, but what truly matters is the inner fruit we bear.

The external, or outer appearance, is what we see in our natural eyes; we only see the person's skin. What kind of eyes do they have, what is their impression, and how do they talk, move, et cetera? You have a limited view of a person, but what is happening in that person's soul? What are their brains and hearts doing to show what defines that person? What fruit are they displaying toward you? It may look like they have the fruits of the spirit but carry the deeds of the flesh. When surrounded by people who bear good fruit, you will start to pick up what they display, which Paul states in 1 Corinthians 15:33: *"Do not* be deceived; *"Bad company corrupts good morals."* Paul also says the deeds of the flesh and the fruits of the Spirit are:

"Now the deeds of the flesh are evident, which are immorality, impurity, sensuality, idolatry, sorcery, enmities, strife, jealousy, outbursts of anger, disputes, dissensions, factions, envying, drunkenness, carousing, and things like these, of which I forewarn you, just as I have forewarned you, that those who practice such things will not inherit the kingdom of God. But the fruit of the Spirit is love, joy, peace, patience, kindness, goodness, faithfulness, gentleness, and self-control; against such things there is no law. Now those who belong to Christ Jesus have crucified the flesh with its passions and desires." (Galatians 5:20-24).

It is through love that We belong to Christ. We walk in the love of Christ, which develops our character and image of God. The gift is how we're given to utilize it, such as teaching, pastoring, prophesying, etc. Love embodies all the fruit. Why work the deeds when we can bear fruit? The more we behold Him, the more our flesh dies. Love isn't something we earn, but we do it for the One who gave His love to us. Beholding the truth looks like acknowledging what Jesus did on the cross for us. His Spirit is the same Spirit that rose Jesus from the dead. The issue is that I believe people don't fully acknowledge Christ but instead acknowledge that we must go through spiritual activities (work-based) to grow in Christ. We place our faith in prayer, spiritual disciplines, and the Word, not looking at Christ. Looking at Christ is when grace is poured out. Looking at anything else stops the flow of grace. Grace is like the water poured out on the plant to grow. It's a perspective we must change to look at Him according to His Word.

Unearthing the Roots: Overcoming Fear, Condemnation, and Stress to Bear Good Fruit

That is the process of looking at Him; we become more sanctified by becoming like Him. If you say you're under grace and yet still live in sin, it would instead be called false mercy. God is merciful, but grace isn't poured out, not because He doesn't want to; it's how the person sees Christ from the wrong perspective. One of the reasons would have to be the specific theology that affects our walk. Many would come to other believers, saying they needed to get right with God because they were taught in a condemning way. Condemnation is nonexistent when you're in Jesus Christ (see Romans 8:1). Having no condemnation means getting rid of the penalty of sin. Jesus approves of you after you have sinned, but not in the way you continue to sin. It's to help you escape that situation through repentance and acknowledging His ways. Yet, it is also to believe we shouldn't be living in condemnation, even when we sin in our walk. Sin is what produces shame, guilt, and condemnation. The difference between living in condemnation is when we make a mistake and our parents yell at us for what we did. Repentance is vital to changing our minds and not continuing to sin. Apostle Paul says we should not sin because we're made alive with Christ, who is the perfect advocate.

Imagine pouring water into a drain. The water can easily flow through the drain. However, think about the nasty stuff in the gutter, like mold, hair, and debris. The water may still flow depending on how much waste is in the way, but it can also cause a blockage if the way the water is processed is slow and dirty. It goes both for sin and doctrine. Doctrine isn't a sin, but some views we hold can block what God wants to do in our lives. How we look and behold Him determines how we can see Him rightly. We tend to fear what God will do to us because of what He'll think of us. Yes, He has emotions, but His Son has paid for your sins once and for all. We sin, feel condemned, and believe God will shoot His lightning toward us.

And so, with a seed, a seed must be taken with care. It needs to have the right tools for the seed to grow correctly. We also need to change our roots to bear good fruit.

Deeper in our roots, we have fear, stress, condemnation, and many more that bind us. How we walk is how we show our fruit. According to research, a long period of stress negatively impacts our immune system and physical health.

We become exposed to diseases and other illnesses. We also tend to look away from what Christ did and focus on ourselves and our circumstances. We stop letting the Holy Spirit pour onto us and look away, like a gardener trying to water a plant without looking at the plant area where it needs to be watered.

You may end up pouring the water outside the area of the plant and losing focus. I'm not to say that God is a terrible gardener, and we should shake our fists at the fact that He isn't showing His love towards us as plants; this is just a metaphor. He is the perfect gardener, the vinedresser who prunes the bad fruit in our lives. He wants to make us right.

The Living Word: Nourishing Roots and Enduring in Christ

We must be around Godly people alive in Christ; imagine an environment like believers surrounding us by receiving what others hold. A plant from a forest wouldn't survive in a desert biome. You cannot surround yourself with unbelievers or an unhealthy environment that produces sin. True believers can speak life into you, tend you, and work on you with the Holy Spirit abiding in them. While some unbelievers may talk about death, rustle you, and damage your spirit.

Over time, depending on where we stay, we may die slowly or grow beautifully. Evaluate yourselves; in which area are you producing life? Life is unique; it's alive. Jesus died so we could live in Him. We die within to receive His life. Allow Him to water you and lead you into the environment. It's about surrender as we float in the river without seeing where He leads us. Still, we know the direction is filled with hope and glory, wherever the river goes.

The Holy Spirit is like the rain that reigns on ourselves, and in Jesus, we bear fruit, similar to John 15. Each one, including the Father, has a role in the Trinity, each having its own functions to live a life like His. God is the vinedresser, Jesus is the vine, and the Holy Spirit is the rain poured upon us. God has to uproot the evil and the flesh out of our lives. Our roots need to be grounded in His Word, not in fear. It takes time for a plant to grow, but there is a reward. We aren't a dead plant but a living one after we have died with Christ. Apostle Peter says that our seed is imperishable:

"For you have been born again not of seed that is perishable but imperishable, that is, through the living and enduring word of God" (1 Peter 1:23).

The Word of God is in us. The more we renew our minds to the Word, the more we bear fruit. The Word is like a fertilizer that gives health to the plant. Most importantly, we received the good news of the gospel that the disciples have written and preached. We can never come to a full conclusion on what the gospel is because of God's mysterious ways. However, we can learn more about the truth every day.

Understanding the gospel takes decades upon centuries; it is impossible, but there is so much power when you walk and learn more every day. The Gospel has the power to transform people's lives. The seed given to born-again believers is imperishable through the enduring Word of God. If the seed is not tended rightly, it will never reach the ultimate growth the way God wants it.

Chapter 4: Doctrine with Power

Doctrine: Denominational Differences and Seeking Unity in the Fullness of God

Now that you have an idea of the seed and the Law, what are the drawbacks that we hold that we aren't looking to the fullness of God? What is the fullness of God? Paul says this in the Ephesus Church:

"For this reason, I bow my knees before the Father, from whom every family in heaven and on earth derives its name, that He would grant you, according to the riches of His glory, to be strengthened with power through His Spirit in the inner man, so that Christ may dwell in your hearts through faith; and that you, being rooted and grounded in love, may be able to comprehend with all the saints what is the breadth and length and height and depth, and to know the love of Christ which surpasses knowledge, that you may be filled up to all the fullness of God." (Ephesians 3:14-19).

Notice how Paul says Christ surpasses all knowledge in that you may be filled with God! With the revelation Paul received from God, he bowed down in humility. And in that, you would be rooted and grounded in His love. We have the riches of His glory that manifest in our lives as we become like Him! Of course, sin changes our perspective of Christ in unrighteousness. We may need to look at Christ correctly, but we may also not look at Him rightly due to the culture we have grown up in. Christianity is filled with many denominations in this modern age. For the past 2,000 years since Christ was crucified, the early Church has been one of the spirit-filled movements. Fifty days after Jesus' resurrection, the Holy Spirit was poured on Pentecost day. God has moved each believer to preach the Gospel to the world. Scripture says that 3,000 people were filled with the Holy Spirit. Jesus said they would be His witnesses in Jerusalem, in all of Judea and Samaria, and even in the remotest part of the earth (see Acts 2).

Peter and the disciples were filled, and it birthed the Early Church as we know it today. Doctrine or denomination wasn't a thing before Jesus came around, except for Judaism; everyone witnessed and preached the Gospel of Jesus through many witnesses and manuscripts. The passage was communicated. The simple teaching was the Gospel. Many of us hold this message dearly in our hearts. The gospel is our core foundation for walking in the fullness of Christ. In the past centuries, there has been a growth of Christianity that has started to break up into denominations due to certain beliefs people hold that oppose the foundation of the Gospel.

What I mean is questions about the nature of God, theologically. In Greek, 'theo' means 'God,' the study of God. Scholars have questioned and gone deep into who God is in Christianity—even asking who Jesus is. Where did He come from? This causes a breakup in groups with certain beliefs they carry that most would agree with and some do not.

Considering Jesus, who was the One who birthed the Church, in the same way, Adam has birthed Eve out of the rib. Christ has full authority over the Church. He is the head of the Church, and we're the body. In unity as a body, we partake in communion to remember what He has done. In accordance, we come to hear the Word and to worship Him. Every Church has a particular schedule, but they are mostly the same.

Modern Churches, Heretical Doctrines, and the Historical Development of Denominations

Not all Churches are like this, unfortunately. Some of the modern Churches out there hold heretical doctrines that are blatantly against the Word of God, since what the enemy has been sowing into. There are roughly over 45,000 denominations in Christianity as of 2022. How did we get there when Christianity started as one, being the early Church as one body, one Truth, and ended up with 45,000 denominations? Did we end up looking at Him with our knowledge and instead focusing on the doctrine we have been taught and learned? It's good that we have doctrine; it is part of our foundation. It's part of our lives that we can live righteousness with Him. Theology is how it impacts our lives. In the book of Timothy, there are four passages that Paul wrote to Timothy's Church that support the doctrine we should grow in that I want to add below:

"But the Spirit explicitly says that in later times some will fall away from the faith, paying attention to deceitful spirits and doctrines of demons" (1 Timothy 4:1).

"In pointing out these things to the brethren, you will be a good servant of Christ Jesus, constantly nourished on the words of the faith and of the sound doctrine which you have been following" (1 Timothy 4:6).

"If anyone advocates a different doctrine and does not agree with sound words, those of our Lord Jesus Christ, and with the

doctrine conforming to godliness, if anyone advocates a different doctrine and does not agree with sound words, those of our Lord Jesus Christ, and with the doctrine conforming to godliness," (1 Timothy 6:3).

"All Scripture is inspired by God and profitable for teaching, for reproof, for correction, for training in righteousness;" (2 Timothy 3:16).

Paul's letters are written in the early Church; before any man, every man created a denomination. It was challenging to compile all the New Testament books. No single text was presented as the New Testament in the first two centuries. A historian, Eusebius (AD 263–339), said that many writings must be connected to the original 12 Apostles. Most Christian communities universally have to accept what is a sound doctrine according to the scripts that were presented. It took roughly 367 years to finally compile the 27 books with the help of Athanasius, a bishop of Alexandria, who wrote a letter that year.

However, before completing the 27 books, the four gospels were Matthew, Mark, Luke, and John. The four books were significant to the culture at the time. The issue, however, was that there were heretic doctrines such as Gnotisicsm that John had to face when writing his three books, which were likely to be reported to the Ephesian Church with other false prophets, antichrists, and many other heretical teachings.

The Book of 2nd John addresses the issue of people who deny the incarnation of Christ, which aligns with the teachings of Gnosticism. These individuals were influenced by syncretism, a blending of different beliefs and practices, and adhered to ascetic practices that rejected the idea of God taking on human form. This situation parallels what the Colossian Church had experienced. Syncretism also gave rise to a teaching called Animism, which involved worshipping nature. In response to these challenges, the Apostle Paul wrote a letter to clarify the true nature of God to the Colossian Church. This letter demonstrated God's faithfulness to the Church.

Paul emphasized that Jesus is the head of the body, as mentioned in Colossians 1:18. However, the Church in Colossae had deviated from this truth and had begun to worship angels instead. While worship can provide a profound encounter with the divine, Paul identified that these visions and experiences can lead to egotistical delusions rooted in worldly desires.

Misinterpretation of Scripture and Heretical Beliefs—The Need for Proper Understanding and Discernment

The whole point of the doctrine and the central biblical beliefs is to see that what we're meant to carry is His birth, power, death, burial, resurrection, ascension, His right throne, and to see Him rightly as our High Priest. In Church History, there were people who would twist the doctrine of Christ into this term called the 'Antichrist.' This is not some crazy one-person antichrist who most dispensationalists believe will destroy the world (or maybe a common belief heard from others and not looking at scripture carefully). The antichrist is denying Christ.

One prevalent issue with many current doctrines that have gained widespread acceptance is that they fail to perceive the true nature of Christ accurately. This lack of understanding can hinder a proper understanding of the significance of John 3:16, which happens to be one of the most well-known and widely quoted verses in the Bible.

John 3:16 states, *"For God so loved the world that he gave his one and only Son, that whoever believes in him shall not perish but have eternal life."* This verse encapsulates the essence of God's love and redemption for humanity. It emphasizes that God's love is so immense and profound that He willingly sacrificed His Son, Jesus Christ, to express His love for the world. This sacrificial act aimed to offer humanity a path to salvation and eternal life through faith in Jesus.

However, the true significance of John 3:16 can be obscured or misinterpreted when Christ is not seen in the proper light. Some doctrines may downplay or distort the divinity of Jesus, diminishing His role as the Son of God and the sole means of salvation. Others may focus solely on His teachings and moral example, neglecting the crucial aspects of His sacrificial death and resurrection.

To fully grasp the message of John 3:16, it is essential to recognize and embrace the truth that Jesus is the Son of God, sent by the Father out of His immeasurable love for humanity. Through His death and resurrection, Jesus provides the way for individuals to be reconciled with God and receive eternal life by placing their faith in Him.

If God so loved the world, He gave His Son to believe. Did people remember the good news that's been revealed in the Gospel, the power it carries? I think many have forgotten and haven't looked at scripture carefully. If we had looked carefully and taken the scriptures seriously, our beliefs would have been transformed by the power of the Holy Spirit. Our minds come up with certain cultural beliefs about Christianity before picking up a Bible.

I'm sure many of you have grown up. The Church has experienced a God who's angry every time you have sinned, and then when you look at the scripture, you see a clearer picture of the Father. I was one of them. I didn't realize until I decided to follow Christ and went deep into scripture that I started to see the Father in His loving, merciful ways. Context is super important when it comes to scripture. Some people read the word literally without looking at the proper context of what goes on. Others may take the meaning out of the author who wrote the book called 'Exegesis.' The opposite is called 'Eisegesis,' which is to put your senses onto a passage.

For example, in Eisegesis, many of you have heard the verse from Philippians 4:13 that says that we can do all things through Him who strengthens us. It's a valid statement, but it doesn't mean He strengthens us when we do things independently and expect Him to strengthen us. Let's look at the whole context, starting from verses 4:10–14.

"*10 But I rejoiced in the Lord greatly that now at last you have revived your concern for me; indeed, you were concerned before, but you lacked opportunity. 11 Not that I speak from want, for I have learned to be content in whatever circumstances I am in. 12 I know how to get along with humble means, and I also know how to live in prosperity; in any and every circumstance, I have learned the secret of being filled and* *going hungry, both of having abundance and suffering need. **13** I can do all things through Him, who strengthens me. **14** Nevertheless, you have done well to share with me my affliction."*

The context behind these four passages is that Paul humbly comes before God. In Philippians, Paul was going through a trial in prison to rejoice in every circumstance and find joy in Christ. It's learning to rejoice before the Lord and receive His grace to power us. Not to be strengthened on our own, for instance, by working in our businesses. It's about the motives that count.

In the example of business, we use Him as a source of a bridge to completing our goals. There is a distinct difference between letting the Lord work in your business and using Him to build it. We aren't supposed to use Christ as a bridge to finishing our goals. It's not our business; it's His business to glorify and advance the Kingdom of God. The Holy Spirit counsels us to make the right choices to take that step of faith and sacrifice what is needed to grow, not in the business aspect but in what we need to lay down. That is what it looks like to surrender.

Next, people use the verses out of context to relate their experiences and define their views on theology. We try to interpret our meanings and misunderstand what the Bible means. It becomes more self-centered than Christ-centered.

Also, when Christianity was born, it was influenced by Ancient Greek philosophers who birthed the Roman Catholic Church and divided the denominations into what we have today, also known as "classical theology ."

Classical theology is seeing the traditional and foundational understanding of God through religious doctrines based on early Christian theologians, emphasizing the Trinity, the Incarnation of Christ, and salvation through faith. It's about the fundamental beliefs that've been passed down for centuries. Now the difference is that yes, this is what we believe in. It's more significant to consider how God sees us as sons and daughters, and I believe people miss that piece. You know a lot about theology but don't have a real relationship with God. It's just like knowing President Biden but not knowing him relationally. We believe he's the president; he holds authority and power, but there's no personal connection.

We see many doctrinal topics nowadays; some or a few have forgotten the accurate Hebraic view of God, also known as "biblical theology." Some may believe that God is sovereign and determines every timeline you cannot change, and He wouldn't be seen as a Father. One time, I visited a Jesus Club in High School, and one reformed believer prayed and believed that *"if it's God's will for them to go to hell, then it would be for God's glory."* Does it sound like the Father in Heaven, whose biggest desire is for us to be called sons and daughters of the Kingdom before even the Heavens and Earth were created? Well, the book of Romans says otherwise:

"For you have not received a spirit of slavery leading to fear again, but you have received a spirit of adoption as sons, by which we cry out, "Abba! Father!" (Romans 8:15)

I encourage you to look into more Hebraic thought. Westerners have traditionally accepted Greek-influenced versions of how they viewed the Bible through their philosophy, but not in the sense of Israel's philosophy. It was broken down from denomination to denomination to now having over 45,000 denominations; perhaps some are unbiblical, which I'll explain later in this chapter.

Moving back to the context of the Bible, the whole point of the Gospel is to deny yourself, pick up the cross, and follow Him. It's practical. Jesus is the Way, the Truth, and the Life. The more we renew our minds to see what the Word says about us, the more we become like Him. In order to become like Him, we must deny ourselves and die to gain Him. Jesus said this:

"And He was saying to them all, "If anyone wishes to come after Me, he must deny himself, take up his cross daily, and follow Me. For whoever wishes to save his life will lose it, but whoever loses his life for my sake is the one who will save it. For what is a man profited if he gains the whole world, and loses or forfeits himself? For whoever is ashamed of Me and My words, the Son of Man will be ashamed of him when He comes in His glory, and the glory of the Father and of the holy angels. But I say to you truthfully, there are some of those standing here who will not taste death until they see the kingdom of God." (Luke 9:23-27)

Even consider what the enemy tried to do to Jesus in the wilderness. In Matthew 4, Jesus was led up by the Spirit into the wilderness to be tempted by the devil (see Matthew 4:1). A couple of verses in the chapter talk about the devil taking Him to the holy city and having Jesus stand on the pinnacle of the temple. This is what Matthew says:

"Then the devil took Him into the holy city and had Him stand on the pinnacle of the temple, and said to Him, "If You are the Son of God, throw Yourself down; for it is written, 'He will command His angels concerning You'; and 'On their hands, they will bear You up So that You will not strike Your foot against a stone.' Jesus said to him, "On the other hand, it is written, 'You shall not put the Lord your God to the test.'" (Matthew 4:5-7)

Do you see why you have to discern scripture well? The devil used a verse from Psalm 91:11 to trick Jesus into jumping off the temple, believing the Angels would save Jesus' fall. Then Jesus knew from the scripture that we should not test the Lord. Notice how there shouldn't be any contradiction in the passage? The more we read and see what the Bible says, the more we can see God clearly. There are even cults that are heretical in modern days. Some groups claim to be Christian but deny one or more of the essentials of the Christian faith. Mormons and Jehovah's Witnesses are examples. We need more wisdom and discernment from our heavenly Father, who can protect us from false spirits.

Christianity's Evolution: From Constantine to Denominational Differences

One of the most significant changes throughout Christianity after the end of the Early Church was Constantine and the Roman Empire, which introduced the Roman Catholic Church that we know today. In AD 312, Constantine converted to Christianity. He may have become a true believer or wanted to unite the Roman Empire. One decision the Emperor made impacted millions of people in the Roman Empire and led them to convert to Christianity. It changed the whole world. Then, the West and East of the Roman Empire split, with the West holding the tradition of Roman Catholicism and the East holding the Eastern Orthodox Church due to a mix of disagreements and political conflicts.

As the division increased, the rise of denominations over the past centuries within the Christian faith decided to create the Protestant Reformation to reform the Roman Catholic Church during the 16th century, which emerged as the four major divisions: Luthern, Reformed, Anabaptist, and Anglican. Over time, it has been split into those four divisions due to the different views inspired by the denominations. The Lutheran Church was named after Martin Luther, whose teachings were the central source of religious authority, in which salvation is received through faith and not works. In the Methodist circle, John Wesley inspired others to learn how to look for methods for spiritual growth. Presbyterians are taught to grow in Church leadership, which, the Greek word for *"elder,"* is *'presbuteros.'* Baptists emphasized the significance of believers' baptisms.

Each denomination has a slight difference in doctrine; some believe that in Calvinism, God determines everything and that we have no free will. The response to Calvinism, the Arminisms, believes that we have the free choice to do whatever we want, and it is up to us to believe in Jesus for what He has done. Other teachings introduced the outcome of Israel, the pre-tribulation vs. post-tribulation rapture, and the spiritual gift that the Pentecostals heavily emphasized, the Holy Spirit. The whole point of these divisions is to see what is consciously right for the believer based on an honest, Godly, and true opinion. It is not to see what Christ is because Christ is the same yesterday, today, and forever.

It is fascinating to observe that God Himself actively seeks out individuals, even if they may appear theologically incorrect from our human perspective. He extends His grace and reaches out to people within various denominations, regardless of how they may align with our theological understanding. What truly matters to God is not the extent of one's theological correctness but rather whether a person is genuinely walking with Christ according to the teachings of the Bible.

God is not concerned with one's Christian background or the number of years spent attending Church. These external factors hold no significance for Him. The Bible, which God divinely inspires, serves as a guide for believers. It contains teachings and wisdom imparted by God and human authors who wrote the books of the early Church and the Old Covenant.

2 Timothy 3:16 highlights the divine origin and purpose of the Scriptures. It states that all Scripture is God-breathed, meaning God Himself inspires it. The verse emphasizes that the Bible is not simply a human creation but a product of divine influence. It further states that the Scriptures are valuable for teaching, rebuking, correcting, and training in righteousness. In other words, the Bible serves as a comprehensive guide for believers, offering instruction, correction, and guidance to help them live a righteous and upright life. It is a source of wisdom and authority that believers can rely on to understand God's will and align their lives with His teachings.

A variety of denominations fit our standards through a preference for worship or a community of people inspired by the Bible. Without the Bible, how would we present ourselves? Moving forward, my only issue is: are we intentional with what Christ calls us to do? The important thing is that God wants Himself to seek Him relationally.

Perhaps the Church we're in isn't suitable for us. Or perhaps we aren't being intentional with ourselves and rather sit on our phones throughout Church service every Sunday and throughout the week; we're too "busy" not to get to know Him more and more every day. Even those whose hearts are hardened by the fact that it's not just the doctrine or denomination we're in, but that pastor's influence of unbiblical doctrine may cause hurt in the body and create division.

To say that God is an angry God who is mad at us means that every time we sin, we believe He doesn't see us as worthy. Some may turn to the pleasures in the world to comfort us and walk away from the faith due to a lack of understanding of our Father-God. It's important how we present ourselves in Christ and how He tells us what to do in the loving way Christ has shown us to walk in. We have to remind ourselves of Exodus 34:6, the nature of God that He describes about Himself.

Christianity's Triumphs and Challenges: From Persecution to Faithful Intentionality

As believers, it is crucial to understand that we must unite in our core beliefs. These essentials of faith revolve around believing in Jesus as the One sent by God, daily repentance, and remembering the profound sacrifice He made for us. Our response to His love involves prayer, fasting, and seeking His presence in the secret place, not as a means to earn or work for His love but as a genuine expression of our devotion. If you aren't connecting with God relationally in those practices, it's meaningless. You must check the motives and seek His love and passion for you.

Christianity has faced challenges throughout its long history as some individuals have sought to distort its message by incorporating human influence and cultural practices. Nevertheless, Christianity remains one of the most significant foundations established in the past 2,000 years. It continues to hold immense relevance and importance, providing a solid framework for believers to build their lives upon.

As a body, we have successfully seen more growth than any man-made religion because of God. Consider Nero in 60 AD. He blamed the Christians who burnt one-third of the Roman Empire when he was the one who called the fire. Then, the Romans started attacking Christianity with heavy persecution, destroying Jeruselum's temple. In this age, the Church has been more victorious than ever, and I am excited to see what God will do in this world.

The Church is never shaken. The enemy has been defeated; Christ will return as a Bridegroom, and we will see Him soon. We cannot let our wrong view of doctrine fill us with fear about the world and what will happen. Yes, the world has worsened, but the Church is far greater than ever. Why let our focus on doctrine influence us when we should see what Jesus talks about in the correct context, including how history has been run for the past 2,000 years? Our foundation is in Christ. We don't allow scripture to fit our personal struggles, when instead He wants you to help you overcome the struggles with Him.

Don't let the influence of culture define how you should see God. Now, the encounters and effects in our lives are what shape our beliefs and how we behave. We go to Church every Sunday and are not in tune with God during worship.

One of the issues nowadays is that people aren't being intentional with the Lord. It is easier to see things that are natural than the supernatural. God helps us understand Him through the Word and our relationship with Him.

The Limitations of Physical Sight: Discerning with Spiritual Eyes

For instance, if you are dating someone, it is much easier to love and be loved by the person because it's physically and naturally in front of our eyes. In the book of Genesis, when God created Eve, He intended her to be a suitable partner for Adam, establishing a natural and harmonious relationship between them. It is important to note that God's physical presence was not directly before Adam during this act of creation. If God were to manifest Himself fully in His glory, it would be overpowering and potentially fatal for human beings. This is illustrated in the story of Moses, where he was permitted to see God's presence but could only witness His back and not His face.

"The Lord said to Moses, 'I will also do this thing of which you have spoken; for you have found favor in My sight, and I have known you by name.' Then Moses said, 'I pray You, show me Your glory!' And He said, 'I Myself will make all My goodness

pass before you and will proclaim the name of the Lord before you, and I will be gracious to whom I will be gracious and will show compassion on whom I will show compassion.' But He said, 'You cannot see My face, for no man can see Me and live!' Then the Lord said, 'Behold, there is a place by Me, and you shall stand there on the rock; and it will come about, while My glory is passing by, that I will put you in the cleft of the rock and cover you with My hand until I have passed by. Then I will take My hand away, and you shall see My back, but My face shall not be seen.'" (Exodus 33:17-23)

In response, God assured Moses that He would allow His goodness to pass before him and proclaimed His name, demonstrating His graciousness and compassion as He saw fit.

However, God made it clear to Moses that no human could see His face and live because of His overwhelming holiness and divine nature. Instead, God offered Moses a special opportunity. He directed Moses to stand on a rock in a designated place near Him. As God's glory passed by, He would place Moses in the cleft of the rock, covering him with His hand for protection. Once God passed by, He would remove His hand, allowing Moses to glimpse His back but not His face. This passage reveals the reverence and awe-inspiring nature of God's presence. While Moses was granted a unique encounter, God's full glory was veiled to ensure the preservation of human life. It emphasizes the transcendence of God and the limitations of human beings in comprehending the entirety of His divine essence.

Moses was interceding with God to see His glory. It was then that the glory of God came in, and only Moses saw God's back and not His face. Possibly, it was due to not revealing the Messiah later, or His glory was so strong that Moses could have died and God was merciful. It wasn't that Moses saw God naturally, but with his spiritual eyes. In our human nature, it is easy to be persuaded by the good things we see in our eyes. Unfortunately, some scholars see this passage as anthropomorphism (a figure of speech or figuring out how God works according to human understanding). This passage is a literal event, not a fantasy or an imagination.

Eve even saw the fruit pleasing to her eyes and ate it. We grow up seeing what is acceptable to our eyes and ears, resulting in sin. I'm not saying that watching a movie at the movie theater is a sin. That isn't true. I don't believe everything secular is terrible, but we should know what is *blatantly* a sin— and know what we are consuming more, the secular content or God? However, God wants us to have a joyful life and not be monks who separate themselves from the physical world, considering it bad or just sinful. I believe it's important to separate ourselves to pursue the Lord.

We are only set apart from the world of sin, which is sanctification. However, be aware of what we consume that doesn't bring life. We have to be mindful of the flesh that leads us to do what isn't blatantly right.

The Authenticity of Love: Preaching the Gospel with Grace and Truth

God's love extends to all people, but He dislikes the sin that resides within them. I believe that when it comes to preaching the gospel, people tend to shame the person instead of encouraging them that God was naked on the cross for their shame, so that we would walk in freedom. Therefore, when representing Christ, it is essential to do so with the power of His grace, acknowledging that none of us are perfect but are recipients of God's grace.

Instead of relying solely on our efforts to understand and convey the message, allowing the Holy Spirit to guide and move within our hearts is vital. Unfortunately, there are instances where individuals preach the Gospel with hate, leaving a negative impression on unbelievers and pushing them further away. These experiences can lead to misunderstandings and perpetuate the idea that Christianity is a religion that should be avoided.

I have heard stories of young children being influenced by their friends or families, resulting in hurtful jokes about the LGBT community and even leading to their expulsion from school. Making cruel jokes about someone is not Christ-like; it is a sinful behavior that goes against the teachings of love and compassion. The essence of the Gospel is about repentance and turning away from evil. Bringing sons and daughters back to the Father.

One challenge lies in the modern world's tendency to reject biblical teachings and instead validate sinful behavior. Acknowledging the struggle individuals may face while adhering to what the Bible says is paramount. By denying or justifying their sin, they may miss the opportunity to experience the Gospel's transformative power. How we should preach the gospel comes with authenticity. Let us be more authentic as we walk in Christ when we evangelize and become relational. It is to share our testimonies of how God has redeemed and cleansed us of our sins. People can tell if you're genuine, and it comes from not the heart of man but Christ. You establish a connection with the stranger you just met in the street. I hear testimonies where even an *"I love you"* can tear a person up who has never received a genuine response compared to others who aren't as true. Many will say they love you, but do not back it up with action. The Holy Spirit is in the person who speaks life into others. Jesus was the only man who truly backed up His actions with love by dying on the cross for us.

The love is demonstrated in the same way Christ has shown His love towards us: while we were sinners, Christ came and died for us (see Romans 5:8). Think about the people who want to hear that kind of love, but their hearts are broken. We live in a broken, fallen world, and a revival is breaking out in areas God is moving in. The Church's awakening and renewal have occurred in the last few decades. Currently, the Church is shifting so that people question what God is doing in the world. For instance, approximately 30,000 Muslims are converted to Christianity daily. It is crucial to convince Muslims that God isn't a God of works but of faith alone. Christianity is the only religion we don't have to work for, while the rest of the religions are Law and works-based. As well as believing that we need to *earn* God because He sees us as unworthy. Therefore, how we present Christ determines how we walk in His fullness when we walk in the power of grace and impact the world.

The Influence of Beliefs: Shaping Lives through Example and Access to Wisdom

It is important to consider our influence on others, including our future children, when it comes to expressing our theology. Whether or not you plan on having kids, your beliefs and actions will always impact someone, regardless of their age, in comparison to yours. You will be a leader in someone's eyes.

When it comes to parents who have faith, the way you raise your child will inevitably be shaped by your beliefs and intentions. This principle applies not only to matters of faith but also to various aspects of life, such as teaching someone how to drive, demonstrating appropriate behavior at the table, or treating one another with respect.

Even in the intimate setting of the bedroom, when you gather with young children to conclude the day with prayer, your child will observe and absorb how you engage in prayer. The words you choose, like addressing God as "Dear God," can shape your child's perception of God as a dear and loving presence. Similarly, expressing gratitude for the things God has done in your life, whether it be for the sacrifice of the cross, the home you own, or the food you have, will teach your child that God is the source of blessings and provisions in your life.

Even in this modern age, it's interesting how much influence has been poured into this world regarding social media. There has been a shift in our society, where people can post based on what they have learned in the past. And how accessible it is for those searching for a "Pink Fairy Armadillo." You think, what the heck is a "Pink Fairy Armadillo? And why is he bringing this up?"

The animal is just an example of how easy it is to find something online that not even one percent would know about.

Now, you are the only person who knows that there is an animal called a "Pink Fairy Armadillo." Or how you wouldn't expect to stumble into an animal like that on the internet. Isn't it wild that we have that much access? In the same way, we can access the Father with His heavenly wisdom, which is far more fantastic than what man has created. There is power when it comes to the Holy Spirit to guide us in becoming more like the Son.

The Importance of Repentance and Discernment in Our Faith Journey

Repentance is one of the biggest keys to growing more in Christ, as I learned that Christ surpasses all knowledge and covers His love for us. It's biblical, and it's needed in our lives to grow. It's like your friend goes to a restaurant and he can't explain how great the food is and tells you to see it for yourself. Now, one of the most significant heretical issues we hear about is Universalism. People have questioned if God is so loving and good to us, and we sit there and think, *"Why would God send us to hell if He's loving?"* It's not that God sends evil people to hell; it's because there has to be a price to pay. One sin equals one penalty. If you were to be ticketed by an officer for parking in the wrong spot in Seattle, you would need to pay the fee. And Jesus, who was perfect in the flesh, paid the spiritual price that no man could have paid, forever. And in order to acknowledge the power of His blood that washes us and makes us brand new, understand that Jesus has often said that the Kingdom of God is at hand. Paul even wrote in Romans, saying:

"That if you confess with your mouth Jesus as Lord and believe in your heart that God raised Him from the dead, you will be saved; for with the heart a person believes, resulting in righteousness, and with the mouth he confesses, resulting in salvation." (Romans 10:9-10).

The Bible verse you mentioned is from Romans 10:9–10. In this passage, the Apostle Paul explains the process of salvation and the role of faith in it.

The verse states, "That if you confess with your mouth Jesus as Lord and believe in your heart that God raised Him from the dead, you will be saved." Here, Paul emphasizes two key components of salvation: confession and belief.

Firstly, *"confessing with your mouth Jesus as Lord"* means openly declaring and acknowledging Jesus as the supreme authority in your life. It involves verbally affirming and proclaiming your faith in Jesus as the Son of God and the Lord over every aspect of your life.

Secondly, *"believing in your heart that God raised Him from the dead"* refers to having a deep, genuine faith in the resurrection of Jesus Christ. It involves a heartfelt conviction that Jesus died on the cross for our sins and was resurrected by God, triumphing over death and sin. Paul goes on to explain the significance of these actions, stating, *"For with the heart a person believes, resulting in righteousness, and with the mouth he confesses, resulting in salvation."* Belief in the heart leads to righteousness, which means being made right with God through faith in Jesus. Confession with the mouth leads to salvation, which is the assurance of eternal life and reconciliation with God.

These verses highlight the importance of both internal faith and external confession in salvation. Genuine belief and heartfelt confession are intertwined, and together, they lead to righteousness and salvation. Through faith in Jesus and openly declaring Him as Lord, one can experience the transformative power of God's grace and receive the gift of eternal life.

If you believe that no one has to confess that Jesus is Lord, regardless of where we are or what we are, that God has given us access to go to heaven even with an unrepentant heart. Then, it destroys what the Bible has taught, including the Gospel. It's heretical. What is the point of the Kingdom of God and not repenting of ourselves before He comes? Repentance is vital to entering the Kingdom of God.

We've already forgiven our sins, but we must accept Him in our hearts. And with repentance, we become righteous with the Father as we regard God's Laws highly with the power of His grace. We don't make up our Laws, but look at what He speaks to us in His Word. Significantly, we understand what His Word says.

There is also an authority placed on believers to manage the Church, but it comes back to the point that Christ will always be the head of everything. If we can see what positions and roles we have to play, we must obey what He has called us to do. It is essential to receive and, more importantly, to give what the Holy Spirit gives us. God's wisdom is far greater than man's wisdom. Yes, receiving what man counsels from the body is important; I'm not painting a dualistic view of ignoring the advice of Godly men. But we shouldn't rely on man's wisdom all the time, which substitutes for our relationship with God. We have the knowledge to seek out and look into things that maybe God called us to do. Charles Spurgeon quotes this:

"Discernment is not knowing the difference between right and wrong. It is knowing the difference between right and almost right."

In the same way, we take communion in our time with the Lord; we have to discern His flesh and blood with the bread and wine. In the same way, we have to discern the body, which is the Church, to know what Christ is calling us to do and not be led by what man has to say. Discernment is crucial but must be put in how Christ sees it. How much you measure to God is how we're measured. The Lord spoke this to Samuel, saying:

"But the Lord said to Samuel, "Do not look at his appearance or at the height of his stature, because I have rejected him; for God sees not as man sees, for man looks at the outward appearance, but the Lord looks at the heart." (1 Samuel 16:7)

Embracing Church History and God's Manifestations: Gaining Wisdom from the Past and Aligning with His Spirit

In Church history, it is significant to understand the importance of seeing the mistakes behind our actions. We can look back to see what and how Christ's body has been moving. It's not that the body is backsliding or Christianity is getting worse daily; it's not true. How you view history will impact your walk with God. Understanding our history and our parents, ancestors, and the people who have opened up the denominations today is vital to seeing their perspective. What were the mistakes that people have made to help us grow?

It is unwise to compare our experiences and put our meaning in scripture, but rather to see what the Bible indeed says and believe what God can do in people's lives that may look unnatural. Some people come from backgrounds that have seen real fruit according to the Word and Spirit, yet others would disagree.

I believe everything the Bible says, word for word, and how God calls us to be where He wants us to be. I don't think there is a contradiction, but rather to be aware that just because one verse in the Bible is what we have to hold, doesn't mean we should disregard the other verses and context. I believe we're contradicting ourselves regarding doctrine we may lack knowledge of. Instead, it's all about looking at Him no matter what our knowledge says. Our knowledge should not be centered on everything; we believe it's wise to do so, but Christ is the center of everything. It emphasizes more the transformation of the believer than his knowledge. God doesn't care how righteous you are on the outside. You can look righteous, but your heart isn't correctly positioned; you will fall due to self-righteousness. In the next chapter, I'll explain what righteousness is.

"Let no man deceive himself. If any man among you thinks that he is wise at this age, he must become foolish so that he may become wise. For the wisdom of this world is foolishness before God. It is written, "He is THE ONE WHO CATCHES THE WISE IN THEIR CRAFTINESS," and again, "THE LORD KNOWS THE

REASONINGS of the wise, THAT THEY ARE USELESS." So then, let no one boast about men. For all things belong to you, whether Paul or Apollos or Cephas or the world or life or death or things present or things to come; all things belong to you, and you belong to Christ; and Christ belongs to God." (1 Corinthians 5:18–23).

How to Repent to God for Our Sins and Establish Relationship.

According to Christian beliefs, repentance is essential to seeking forgiveness from God for our sins. Here is a list of ways to repent based on Christian teachings:

1. **Recognize and acknowledge your sins:** Examine your thoughts, actions, and behavior to identify how you have fallen short of God's standards. Believe that He truly died for sins, was buried, and was resurrected on the third day.

2. **Genuine sorrow and remorse:** Develop a sincere and contrite heart, feeling genuine remorse for your sins and how they have hurt your relationship with God and others.

3. **Confess your sins to God:** Approach God in prayer, confessing your sins and expressing your desire for forgiveness. Be specific and honest, acknowledging each sin by name.

4. **Seek forgiveness from God:** Humbly ask God for His forgiveness, recognizing that forgiveness is a gift of His grace and not something we can earn on our own merit.

5. **Repentance through turning away:** After confessing your sins, commit to turning away from them. It involves a

genuine desire to change your thoughts, attitudes, and behaviors to align with God's will.

6. **Make restitution:** Whenever possible, take steps to make amends for the harm you have caused to others as a result of your sins. It can involve apologizing, seeking forgiveness, or making reparations.

7. **Embrace accountability and community:** Seek the support and guidance of a trusted spiritual mentor, pastor, or fellow believers who can provide accountability and help you grow in your repentance journey.

8. **Study and meditate on God's Word:** Engage in regular Bible study and reflection to better understand God's principles, His forgiveness, and the transformative power of His grace.

9. **Develop a prayerful life:** Develop a consistent prayer life, seeking God's guidance, strength, and wisdom to resist temptation and grow in righteousness.

10. **Live a transformed life:** As evidence of true repentance, strive to live a life that reflects the teachings of Jesus Christ. Seek to love God and others, practicing forgiveness, humility, compassion, and obedience to God's commands.

Remember that repentance is not a one-time event but an ongoing process of turning away from sin and growing closer to God. It is a journey of continual renewal and reliance on God's grace and mercy.

"Therefore bear fruits in keeping with repentance, and do not begin to say to yourselves, 'We have Abraham for our father,' for I

say to you that from these stones God is able to raise up children to Abraham." (Luke 3:8)

Chapter 5: The Gift of Righteousness

Embracing Righteousness: Experiencing God's Transforming Power and Shifting Our Moral Identity

Righteousness is one of the critical aspects of living for Christ. We concluded the last chapter on how we can see that the world has an influence, including the denominations broken up and how the body is growing more every day. Furthermore, even the sinful world can damage the Church and cause it to go astray, missing God's fullness. Righteousness is a gift that we can tap into because of what He did on the cross for us.

"For if, by the transgression of the one, death reigned through the one, much more those who receive the abundance of grace and of the gift of righteousness will reign in life through the One, Jesus Christ. (Romans 5:17)

Furthermore, righteousness can be understood as a state of alignment with God, where our thoughts, actions, and intentions are in harmony with His divine will. Through our acceptance of Jesus Christ as our Savior, we can establish a profound connection with the Father. Jesus, being fully human and fully divine, holds authority over the earthly realm and heaven.

In the context of righteousness, it is crucial to understand that it encompasses more than just a spiritual state of alignment. It also involves living a life that adheres to moral principles, uprightness, and justice. This moral dimension of righteousness calls us to act by God's standards and values, treating others with fairness, compassion, and respect. It encourages us to pursue justice, advocate for the oppressed, and stand against injustice and inequality.

We try to mirror God's character and bring respect to His name by embracing righteousness. It is a never-ending process of change and growth in which we allow the Holy Spirit to work inside us, transforming our desires, attitudes, and actions. Righteousness becomes a guiding principle that impacts our choices, relationships, and decisions, aligning them with God's flawless and just nature.

It is important to note that our righteousness is not achieved through our own efforts or merits alone. Rather, it results from God's grace and our faith in Jesus Christ. Jesus bridged the gap between humanity and God through His sacrifice on the cross, offering us forgiveness, redemption, and the opportunity to be made righteous in His sight. We are clothed in His righteousness through our faith in Him and our acceptance of His gift of salvation.

The crucifixion of Jesus on the cross paved the way for us to attain right standing with the Father. We gain access to this state of righteousness once we embrace and have faith in Jesus' sacrifice. It is worth mentioning that individuals who attend Church yet have not fully experienced the complete manifestation of God's power still maintain their right standing with God. However, some may have developed a distorted perception of the Father. There is a tendency to doubt what God can do for us.

I'll touch on the law of morality in a few chapters. But under the law of morality, we're given rules that make us morally correct. We grow up in environments where we know what is morally right. One instance is wearing clothes is required because we don't want to see nakedness from other people. That one is very clear. It is immoral and breaks the law if a man is naked in public.

The Gospel is not simply about receiving moral rights but about the Man who gave His life for us. Righteousness is traded with our own lives for His instead. Why? To be righteous, you must follow every moral law God has given you. And it is nearly impossible to do so. Saul, the only Pharisee who seriously devoted His life to His work, might have done it, but yet he has at least missed one mark. Still, he didn't acknowledge the finished work of the cross until later, when he met Jesus and became Apostle Paul (see Acts 9).

The Bible verse that supports the concept mentioned is 2 Corinthians 5:17. It states:

"Therefore, if anyone is in Christ, the new creation has come: the old has gone, the new is here!"

This verse emphasizes that when a person experiences the transformative power of being born-again and accepting Christ, they become a new creation. The Holy Spirit speaks to their hearts, revealing their true identity in Christ.

As individuals embrace their new identity, their old lifestyles and sinful patterns change profoundly. For instance, someone who was once trapped in the grip of drug addiction may find deliverance and freedom through God's intervention. The Holy Spirit then guides them and reminds them that they are no longer defined by their past addictions. They are now a new creation in Christ, liberated from the bondage of their former habits.

It is important to note that the Holy Spirit's work is not limited to breaking free from addiction alone. He continually shapes and molds believers, leading them away from any patterns of sin or destructive behaviors. The Holy Spirit is a constant reminder of their true identity in Christ. It empowers them to live in alignment with that identity, making choices that reflect their new nature. Righteousness is what we become when we behold Him every single day.

"For in it the righteousness of God is revealed from faith to faith; as it is written, "But the righteous man shall live by faith." (Romans 1:17)

The Greek word for *'righteousness'* is *'dikaiosýnē'* and it says in the Mounce's definition: *"righteousness, what is right, justice, the act of doing what is in agreement with God's standards, the state of being in proper relationship with God."*

Therefore, when faced with the temptation to retake the same drugs or engage in old sinful patterns, the Holy Spirit prompts believers to resist because those actions contradict who they have become in Christ. The Holy Spirit's guidance serves as a loving reminder that they are no longer bound by their past but are now called to live according to their new identity as children of God. We become to walk in alignment with God and to be in a proper relationship.

Your sense of morality shifted, knowing it wasn't right to take those drugs anymore. You start to see that they have no benefit because you have found something even more remarkable. God shifts our identity even more into becoming like sons and daughters of the Kingdom, also known as sonship.

Living in Surrender: Embracing Sonship and Fixing Our Gaze on Jesus

The definition of sonship is a relationship between the Son and the Father. Jesus starts to intercede for us on behalf of the Father. And so, to bounce off the last chapter with doctrine, we shape our views based on what the Holy Spirit does to our lives, not to understand what we see and know. We all have different opinions on Christianity based on the denomination we grew up in. Some of us may lose interest based on the Church we grew up in. That is why God calls us to go elsewhere to fit the standard He wants us to meet. And the Holy Spirit corrects our standards. It doesn't mean that we let the Holy Spirit do everything and sit in our homes doing nothing. We're led by the Holy Spirit when we surrender, as He starts to direct our steps.

The Psalm of David says this:

"Where can I go from Your Spirit? Or where can I flee from Your presence? If I ascend to heaven, You are there; if I make my bed in Sheol, behold, You are there. If I take the wings of the dawn, If I dwell in the remotest part of the sea, even there Your hand will lead me, and Your right hand will lay hold of me." (Psalms 139:7-10)

The mentioned Bible verse, 1 Corinthians 1:30–31, highlights the significance of surrendering to the Holy Spirit and recognizing the central role of Jesus in our lives. It emphasizes that our true wisdom, righteousness, sanctification, and redemption come from God through Christ Jesus.

The verse begins by conveying that we are called to surrender to the Holy Spirit, allowing Him to guide and lead us in every aspect of our lives. It encourages us to hold onto His hand, symbolizing a reliance on His presence and guidance throughout our journey. This surrender to the Holy Spirit is portrayed as essential for a renewed mind.

The concept of a renewed mind is then explained as recognizing that, regardless of our circumstances or location, we always have Jesus with us. The verse emphasizes that Jesus is paramount in our lives, surpassing worldly possessions or achievements. It suggests that even if we were to lose everything, we would still have the presence of Jesus, which is the most valuable and comforting aspect of our existence.

The verse also highlights the importance of understanding the Truth, which is found in God's Word. It encourages seeking God's voice and guidance through His Word, emphasizing the continuous process of renewing our minds through Him. This implies that as we align our thoughts and perspectives with God's truth, our mindset transforms, and we gain a deeper understanding of His ways.

The verse further emphasizes that God does not show favoritism when it comes to His Truth. It asserts that there is no room for boasting or pride before God, as everything we have and are ultimately results from His work in us. The verse references the book of James (James 5), supporting the idea that boasting should be directed towards the Lord, recognizing His grace and provision in our lives.

"So that no man may boast before God. But by His doing, you are in Christ Jesus, who became to us wisdom from God, righteousness, sanctification, and redemption, so that, just as it

is written, "Let him who boasts, boast in the Lord." (1 Corinthians 1:30–31)

And:

"My brethren, do not hold your faith in our glorious Lord Jesus Christ with an attitude of personal favoritism. For if a man comes into your assembly with a gold ring and is dressed in fine clothes, and there also comes a poor man in dirty clothes, and you pay special attention to the one who is wearing the fine clothes and say, "You sit here in a good place," and you say to the poor man, "You stand over there, or sit down by my footstool," have you not made distinctions among yourselves, and become judges with evil motives? Listen, my beloved brethren: did not God choose the poor of this world to be rich in faith and heirs of the kingdom that He promised to those who love Him? But you have dishonored the poor man. Is it not the rich who oppress you and personally drag you into court? 7 Do they not blaspheme the fair name by which you have been called? If, however, you are fulfilling the royal law according to the Scripture, "You shall love your neighbor as yourself," you are doing well. But if you show partiality, you are committing sin and are convicted by the law as transgressors." (James 2:1-9)

A person may look righteous on the outside, as I brought up in 1 Samuel, and people favor men by their outward appearance. Think about it. Many of us have been judges, believing righteousness is based on our work. Some of us have been deceived by the idea that we look at things that are outward. That is, to receive Christ, it is through works and to strive to inherit Him. And for those who aren't living for Christ yet go to Church, they look at those who are righteous in their eyes. I'm not saying everyone isn't unrighteous, but we deceive ourselves by relying on a pastor, not God. Yes, it is essential to receive counsel. Still, we don't receive righteousness until we see that we're righteous before God's eyes. Others compare themselves and favor themselves in their works. We don't boast in our works but in the Lord because He has given us righteousness. It is about loving and honoring your neighbor. But most importantly, it is about allowing God to speak when you lay down your life.

The Call to Love: Embracing God's Commandment of Love and Unity

We must practice righteousness daily and always have it in our daily lives. We have been free from sin and have become slaves of righteousness (see Romans 6:18). If you do not see Truth in your lives, then you haven't entirely laid down your lives. Jesus said this in Matthew:

"Then some Pharisees and scribes came to Jesus from Jerusalem and said, "Why do Your disciples break the tradition of the elders? For they do not wash their hands when they eat bread." And He answered and said to them, "Why do you transgress the commandment of God for the sake of your tradition? For God said, 'Honor your father and mother,' and, 'He who speaks evil of father or mother is to be put to death.' But you say, 'Whoever says to his father or mother, "Whatever I have that would help you has been given to God," he is not to honor his father or his mother.' And by doing so, you invalidated the word of God for the sake of your tradition. You hypocrites rightly did Isaiah prophesy of you:

'These people honor Me with their lips, but their hearts are far away from Me. 'But in vain do they worship Me, teaching as doctrines the precepts of men.'" (Matthew 15:1-9).

Could you imagine we are not honoring one another, if not most, of the Christian culture? We aren't practicing what it is to be right-standing with the Father and missing the key of sonship. God created a family through Abraham to restore our sonship to Him so we can love our brothers and sisters in Christ. It looks like honoring people and blessing those who persecute you. We come into theological arguments that cause so much division in the body that they destroy potential connections because we rely on our understanding rather than what God is trying to tell us.

When we forget, the essence of the Gospel is to love one another as I loved you (see John 13:34). If you continue to say that God doesn't love the way He sees us in our sins, lives, and attitudes, that isn't glorifying Him. Then, we have believed in a lie. He doesn't love our sins, but we think He dislikes us for who we are. It's a lie. It isn't the person, but it's a sin that God hates. God loves the person but hates the sin. We also lie to ourselves to see that we say we love God and hate our brother, yet we believe we're still in the Truth. One of my favorite books in the Bible is 1 John. I believe it is one of the core foundations of our walk. In chapter 4 of 1 John, it says this:

"Whoever confesses that Jesus is the Son of God, God abides in him, and he in God. We have come to know and have believed God has love for us. God is love, and the one who abides in love abides in God, and God abides in him. By this, love is perfected with us so that we may have confidence in the day of judgment,

because as He is, so are we in this world. There is no fear in love, but perfect love casts out fear because fear involves punishment, and the one who fears is not perfected in love. We love because He first loved us. If someone says, "I love God," and hates his brother, he is a liar, for the one who does not love his brother whom he has seen cannot love God whom he has not seen. And this commandment we have from Him, that the one who loves God should love his brother also." (1 John 4:15-21).

Embracing Trials and Finding Hope: The Path to Character and Growth

The Bible verse referenced in the statement is 2 Timothy 1:7, which states:

"For God has not given us a spirit of fear, but of power, love, and a sound mind."

This verse reminds us that fear does not originate from God. Instead, He has endowed us with a spirit characterized by power, love, and self-discipline.

They found themselves entangled in a perception of God as a stern figure, resembling an earthly father who disciplines and punishes a wayward child. Within this framework, they internalized the notion that their previous actions defined the very essence of their being.

However, the truth is that God has always pursued humanity with love, even after the fall of mankind. When we acknowledge this truth and confess that God dwells within us, aligning our actions with His nature is essential. Engaging in behaviors like gossiping contradicts the nature of God, for there is no darkness in Him—only light.

To walk in the fullness of God, we must grasp the depth of His love and not allow past sins, negative experiences, or false beliefs to hinder our progress. God has forgiven us for all these things, and our responsibility is to repent and invite the Lord to transform our minds. Additionally, it is crucial to open ourselves up to the support and guidance of others in our lives.

By embracing God's love, seeking His forgiveness, and allowing His transformative power to work within us, we can break free from the bondage of fear and walk in the fullness of His grace.

You are a son. You are righteous. You are in Christ. It's the truth. There are a hundred things that God is telling you, and it's up to you if you believe them. It's about taking action to consider what we seek in ourselves through Him. Most people think it's about accepting the way life is. We're tossed around by life, and we just have to deal with life the way it is. That is not the life we should live; instead, we should become intentional with God in our lives. We must have a Father who can guide us through our lives, knowing that our end goal is Him. Our lives should be a daily worship to Him, no matter where we're at, and He can lift us up. Jesus said, *"Whoever exalts himself shall be humbled, and whoever humbles himself shall be exalted"* (see Matthew 23:12).

We cannot build ourselves up without God; we must see that, in our strength, we cannot get to a spot where God wants us to be. God is waiting for those ready to go through trials and tribulations. Suffering is the key to growth; without suffering, we will not be able to grow in the likeness of His image, and the Church is scared to talk about suffering. Peter says that even if you suffer for righteousness, you are blessed (see 1 Peter 3:14). There is joy behind the suffering. In Romans, it says that through our trials and tribulations, we see that our character shapes.

"Therefore, having been justified by faith, we have peace with God through our Lord Jesus Christ, through whom also we have obtained our introduction by faith into this grace in which we stand, and we rejoice in the hope of the glory of God. Not only this, but we also exult in our tribulations, knowing that tribulation brings about perseverance; and perseverance, proven character; and proven character, hope; and hope does not disappoint because the love of God has been poured out within our hearts through the Holy Spirit who was given to us" *(Romans 5:1–5).*

A Heart Transformed by Truth: Moving Beyond Condemnation and Embracing Righteousness

Upon my reunion with the Lord in the preceding year, I realized that my deepest longing was for a connection with Him. The past experience of succumbing to lukewarmness had left a lasting impact, tarnishing my spiritual journey. I was acutely aware that trials and tribulations would inevitably accompany me, even with Jesus by my side. My knowledge of Scripture was scant, and I yearned to deepen my understanding. My heart burned with an authentic devotion to the Lord, yet I was overly preoccupied with my shortcomings and sins.

120

One of the things growing up as a Christian is this heavy condemnation I've carried. One of my struggles was pornography. Although I was set free in 2021, before then, it was one of my biggest strongholds, and it was condemning knowing how mad the Father would be at my sin. The fact that I knew that I didn't want to live a lifestyle made me question what would happen to my future friendships and relationships. The more I behold my behavior, the more I'll continue to sin. In my trials and tribulations, I wanted to get so free because of my sincere heart.

What God does to those who believe in the Son is that the deepest part of our hearts becomes sincere before Him. It is also called righteousness. The issue that most believers have is that they aren't beholding the truth. What is the truth? The Gospel is the truth. You would ask yourself, *"Why would God say I'm a son, righteous, and pure before His eyes, and yet I'm still in my sin?"* Because deep down in your heart, you want God, but you're looking at things from the wrong perspective. Now, we don't completely ignore sin; we see it as a warning to not do it again. Instead, we look at what God has done for us, setting us free, then we look back to remember what sin has done in our lives, and then we remember the testimony that we are witnesses of God's goodness towards us. He set us free from bondage, and we continue to walk in holiness with the Lord.

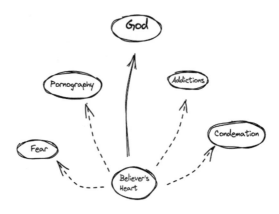

I drew this graph to show an example of a believer's heart. Notice how the arrow towards God is bold compared to the other dotted arrows pointing at the person's sins. Their hearts are deep in God, but they look toward the issues of their lives. More so, it's not the issue of corruption, but it's what they are beholding. I met men who want God with sincerity and to be free, but look at their problems more than Jesus. You can tell a person by their sincerity in general how much they want to get free. Pornography addiction is the same as drug addiction because, other than the deepest part of the heart, they are conscious of their behavior. Still, in other cases, they enjoy the source that gives them instant gratification.

Imagine you look at this graph; you may face other things holding you back from the fullness of God. Perhaps it's not what I listed as an example, but maybe you're facing an issue of depression. You may be the person who is facing something that is holding you down on a personal note. James says to confess your sins to another so that you may be healed (see James 5:16).

This verse applies to those who can't find a solution or are in fear of opening up. Most importantly, ask the Holy Spirit what you are struggling with. Then, on that same graph, you can write your little circles and arrows to add what you have been holding on to. Then, cross off those labels and circle God and only Him.

The point of this activation is letting go and recognizing that you are not who you are. Your identity is rooted in God. You don't identify yourself with fear, anxiety, depression, etc. What's worse is that you are looking at those issues more than Jesus when you can just give those issues to Him. He already paid for your sins 2,000 years ago. Your graph would look something like this.

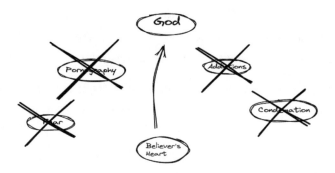

This is what it looks like to see Him as the true and only source of everything. You start to see that these labels aren't who you are or what you are satisfied with. You start to see that sin is not your desire or portion. God's design is to sanctify you and free you from your sins through repentance and renewal.

The more you lay down your life for Him, the more you will be transformed. Jesus didn't say to lay down thirty percent of your life and continue to do whatever you want with it. It's laying down everything you have in your life. One hundred percent. Jesus says, *"Whoever wishes to save his life will lose it, but whoever loses his life for My sake, he is the one who will save it"* *(Luke 9:24).*

Experiencing the Fullness of God: Surrendering All to Find Rest and Transformation

It's important to know what you're holding on to because it seems dear to you that you know that God is calling you to let go of the thing you hold. You understand that the pain you've carried for years isn't giving you the peace you always wanted. Interestingly, for those unbelievers, the deepest part of their hearts is saying they don't want God. People have come to understand that God has already forgiven your sins. It's about whether you have accepted Him into your life or not. And to those who feel so empty inside, simply give that pain to Him.

Perhaps you, as the reader, have possibly never met Jesus in your life. I want to challenge you to intently ask Him with your heart and accept Him into your life. He has died on the cross, so you can have life in Him. Not your understanding of life, not your definition of peace, love, and joy. But something more significant is far greater than you think it may look.

The source of love is found in God and only in Him. And to those who grew up in the Church and haven't found true peace, consider Him. If you don't have a relationship with Him, ask Him if you want to start and pursue one. God has been waiting and seeking those who are lost. In earthly relationships, love eludes us. Drugs fail to provide true satisfaction. Other religions and gods cannot offer genuine peace. The praises of man do not hold the key to lasting joy. The sole, vibrant source of all these blessings lies in Jesus alone—the living, active force that brings love, satisfaction, peace, and joy.

Otherwise, your source is temporary, and you can't truly find any greater source than Jesus. Maybe even people who have grown up in the Church and haven't built a strong foundation would lift you. It's about laying down, even your dignity and pride, and seeing that there is something more than we think. And it is the blood of Jesus that washes and cleanses us of any unrighteousness. You might ask, *"Do we separate ourselves from the world?"* No, the point is building a relationship with God and bringing people into that relationship.

In that, we continue to see who our source is, the more we trust Him and renew our minds. Righteousness is an action taken by faith, and we let the grace of God transform us. Faith does not save us, but grace does (see Ephesians 2:8). Grace saves us, and how do we obtain it? It's *through* faith in Christ alone that we receive this gift. It is by laying down and humbling yourself before the King, not just seeing Him as a savior. It's a simple gift. If it was your birthday, you know work did not earn your gifts.

One of the issues with our motivations is reserving only a spot in Heaven. Christianity isn't just accepting Jesus, being forgiven, doing your best, and going through life just the way we think it is. That is not the Gospel. The Gospel says that He has given His life, His power, and Himself so that we can also reign in life with Him. It was His blood that cleansed us, washed us, and transformed us. Paul said that the blood of Jesus draws us near to Him (see Ephesians 2:13). I was the worst at reading or writing, and I had one of the lowest test scores in math and other subjects. I was disabled in knowing that my speech was terrible. I used to have a huge fear of speaking. I never wanted to talk in front of an audience. Yet, I had so much I could have shared that I wish I had stepped out more.

However, God has restored me. He has healed me of my disabilities; I never even asked to be healed when I was younger. I did not know of His presence; all I knew was that He revealed His glory so that I could walk in the fullness of God. But what is the fullness of God? I explained in the last chapter that in Ephesians, the love of Christ surpasses knowledge so that you may fill up to all the fullness of God (see Ephesians 3:19). How do we receive it? It's to surrender and walk in obedience. Now, do we work for obedience? Not necessarily; it's about knowing what rest is by following Him. Jesus talks about rest in Matthew, explaining how important it is for our souls to be at rest. He says this:

"Come to Me, all who are weary and heavy-laden, and I will give you rest. Take My yoke upon you and learn from Me, for I am gentle and humble in heart, and you will find rest for your souls. My yoke is easy, and my burden is light." (Matthew 11:28-30).

Where have you been in your life that you feel so overwhelmed? His heart is open to helping you grow, but it is up to you if you want to grow into that. You have to lose your dignity to grow every day. Give your dignity to Him. Glory looks like dying for yourself and picking up the cross.

Your flesh needs to die according to the word. Jesus has crucified your flesh (see Galatians 5:24), but do you believe you have died for your sins? Do you believe God wants to transform you into seeing that He is the source of everything? Is He your Savior, or is He your King? Many see Him as the savior who took sin on our behalf, and we're forgiven. It's not to overthink this and feel like you aren't close to Him. But what is He to you after you have been forgiven? To see who He is, you must submit everything you are holding on to that is dear to you to see His glory work in your life. Trust that He can help you get through the struggles you have been facing for years. You are not dead but instead resurrected to life in Him!

The essence of the message is to highlight the importance of relinquishing personal attachments and opening oneself up to God's presence. It encourages individuals to actively seek a relationship with Jesus, who offers forgiveness for their sins and a unique source of love, peace, and joy that cannot be found elsewhere. The path to righteousness involves accepting Jesus as Lord and Savior, cultivating a deep connection with God, adhering to His commandments, embodying love and compassion in our interactions with others, living with integrity, relying on the guidance of the Holy Spirit, seeking forgiveness when needed, and understanding that righteousness is a continuous journey fueled by faith and the grace of God.

Righteousness in Christianity encompasses several key aspects. Firstly, it begins with accepting Jesus Christ as Lord and Savior, acknowledging Him as the Son of God, and personally embracing His sacrificial death and resurrection. It entails confessing one's sins, repenting, and placing faith in Jesus.

Secondly, seeking a personal relationship with God is essential to pursuing righteousness. It involves praying, worshiping, and studying the Bible to align one's heart, mind, and actions with God's will. Regular communion with God helps foster a deeper connection and understanding of His righteousness.

Furthermore, righteousness entails obeying God's commandments and principles outlined in the Bible. It includes adhering to the Ten Commandments and following the teachings of Jesus. By striving to live according to God's standards, individuals demonstrate their commitment to righteous living.

Another vital aspect of righteousness is love, compassion, and kindness towards others. Christianity emphasizes the importance of loving God and one's neighbors. Demonstrating forgiveness, compassion, and serving others reflect God's righteousness and exemplify the teachings of Jesus.

Living a life of integrity and honesty is also integral to righteousness. It means upholding moral values, being trustworthy, and acting with integrity in all areas of life. Personal relationships, professional responsibilities, and daily interactions should all reflect a commitment to righteousness.

Seeking righteousness is not a solo endeavor but is made possible through the indwelling of the Holy Spirit. Christians believe the Holy Spirit empowers believers to live righteously, guiding their decisions and actions. Yielding to the guidance of the Holy Spirit enables individuals to align their lives with God's righteousness.

Repentance and seeking forgiveness are vital steps in the pursuit of righteousness. Recognizing personal shortcomings and sins, individuals humbly seek forgiveness from God and others. Repentance involves avoiding sinful behaviors and embracing God's grace and transformative power.

Lastly, righteousness is viewed as a lifelong journey rather than an instant achievement. It requires perseverance, self-reflection, and continuous growth in faith. Christians understand they are imperfect but rely on God's grace and His transformative work to pursue righteousness.

To summarize, righteousness in Christianity involves accepting Jesus Christ as Lord and Savior, seeking a relationship with God, obeying His commandments, practicing love and compassion, living with integrity, relying on the Holy Spirit, seeking forgiveness, and understanding that righteousness is a lifelong journey fueled by faith and grace.

Chapter 6: Trusting The Father In His Timing

Redeeming Time: Embracing God's Purpose and Salvation

As time goes by, we can spend it for the good of our lives. Time is linear; it is one path. As the universe constantly expands, God's spirit is saving people from the pit of hell. Not that the Father sends people to hell because people are evil, but there needs to be a price to pay. Time is crucial in our lives. And time is sometimes wasted on pointless things, which we regret. Time is something that God is in both the Heavens and Earth. Time comes with a due date, such as, a credit card payment that needs to be made or the bills.

People, for instance, want to achieve their goal of becoming astronauts by the age of thirty. Yet, as in the present time, we continue to battle with our minds with time. They create lies and beliefs about themselves, saying it isn't possible, saying that they are terrible at math, and continuing to complain that they can't become astronauts because of an area they lack.

And I believe people can choose to live in that kind of reality of remaining where they are, not taking the initiative by faith, or not wanting to do anything about it. Stuck. I believe people are walking with leprosy, and it would be impossible for them to grow. You're just stuck; it's just a plateau, and people don't bother to seek the Lord with all seriousness.

We are designed to grow and build something. I speak to those who are unbelievers who haven't found true purpose or to believers who lack in reverence.

The verse mentioned in 2 Corinthians 6:2 (NASB 1995) further reinforces the message. It states, *"For he says, at the acceptable time, I listened to you, and on the day of salvation, I helped you. ' Behold, now is 'the acceptable time,' behold, now is 'the day of salvation.'"*

This verse serves as a powerful reminder of the significance of time in the context of our spiritual journey. It echoes the idea that God is attentive and responsive to our prayers and supplications. The reference to *"the acceptable time"* and *"the day of salvation"* underscores the urgency and relevance of the present moment. Biblically speaking, anyone can evangelize to someone. You don't need to have a certain gift or calling, such as being an evangelist, to preach the gospel. We have the right to preach the good news, but we cannot waste time.

By quoting Isaiah 49:8, the verse emphasizes that God's timing is perfect. It highlights that when we turn to Him, seeking His help and salvation, He is ready and willing to extend His grace and deliverance. The repetition of *"behold, now is"* underscores the immediacy and importance of embracing the present moment for our spiritual well-being. Not just for ourselves but for others as well.

Considering the issues you may have encountered, even to question where life goes when I pass away? How dangerous is it to believe we can fix it ourselves and never understand God's divine plan? Going back to what I was sharing about being "stuck," we have to figure it out on our own but rather walk in humility. I was reminded by a scripture from Proverbs 16:9:

"The mind of man plans his way, but the Lord directs his steps." (Proverbs 16:9)

I will touch on more in the next two chapters of *'The Mind,'* and I want you to really think that God does have a plan for you. God wants to fix you up and give you a purpose so you can spend time with Him forever but also treasuring things on heaven by simply walking like Him according with His Word. Do not burn time with things of pleasure, depression, anxiety, or distracting things that are hindering your purpose in life.

God is the purpose of your life. He holds above all things. Nothing can be above Him. Yet out of His humility, He chooses to love you and wants to spend time with you. He is passionate about you. Believe that He can give you the grace to spend time growing in maturity in Christ. Take advantage of this moment. Believe in Him if you have neglected Him; He is more than faithful to help you in your need. However, the promises that He has planned for us in His timing are possibly one of the most challenging things we face. How do we trust in His timing? We can look at the story of Elijah, who was a man that was used by God to win a contest against the four-hundred Baal prophets, raise a son to life, and many more amazing stories.

We see this story as about someone who is zealous and bold. However, Elijah didn't just have these characteristics. It was spending time with God in the secret place that led Him to conquer. Elijah spent three years in a cave by himself with the Lord, receiving provisions of bread and meat. All alone with the Lord, just to know Him. In those three years, He was being sanctified and transformed by the Spirit to walk in power and conquer the world with God. Often times, we love to seek God's will and will do anything for Him, and He loves that. However, as a loving Father, He takes time to transform you so that you are well prepared for the promises that He has given you so that you won't be hurt.

Navigating Fatherhood: Building Relationships and Cultural Challenges

Time holds immense significance in our lives, shaping our experiences and growth. As I reflect on my journey, I recall moments when I spent time on trivial pursuits, unaware of their true value. While there is certainly room for enjoyment and joy in life, it is crucial to consider how we allocate our time on a daily basis. In our relationship with God, family, friends, and even strangers who are in need of God.

In my youth, I found myself immersed in a video game addiction. It was an idol in my life. Although adolescence is often seen as a time of exploration and youthful exuberance, I struggled to find my true path. I grappled with the weight of understanding my own worth and felt apprehensive about making significant strides forward. During this period, my older brother became a paternal figure, offering guidance and support. I also faced challenges with speech, particularly in my second language, Ukrainian. I lacked in my secondary language, especially within my family.

One of the most arduous hurdles I encountered was the absence of a deep connection with my father. Our relationship was not strained, but it lacked the intimacy I longed for. While my father was often occupied with his trucking business, which he excelled at, our interactions remained somewhat surface-level. In contrast, my brother, who is fluent in English, shared a profound bond with me. The disparity in connections was a source of hardship.

To this day, I deeply admire my earthly father, recognizing his tremendous work ethic and dedication to our family. He has built a successful trucking business and, despite nearing fifty years of age, continues to provide for us. Our family enjoys financial stability, yet it pained me to feel somewhat disconnected from his life during my formative years. However, our relationship has evolved and grown healthier over time.

Navigating the challenges inherent in the Slavic community and its cultural expectations was no easy feat. Nonetheless, I have learned valuable lessons about the importance of time, the significance of familial bonds, and the resilience of relationships.

Slavic parents tend to be stoic and conservative; that's how I grew up in the community. I am not to say that all Slavic people are, but everyone, in every culture, has at one point probably diminished one's feelings to avoid shame or to keep pride in oneself, depending on the motive. As younger kids, we tend to be disobedient to our parents because there is disagreement. We don't want to do what our parents wish. Culturally, parents have had enough with their kids, become stressed, and sometimes have to beat us to understand a point. Kids are rebellious as they grow up and, worse, when they get so immersed in this world. To this degree, even parents cry and are confused about why their kids ended up in the world.

Nurturing the Hearts of Children: Embracing God's Love and Discipline with Grace

We need childlike faithfulness in Christ. In the context of the mentioned verses, Matthew 18:6 and Matthew 18:10, Jesus addresses His disciples and conveys a message regarding the significance of children and their relationship with God.

These verses shed light on our responsibility to treat children with respect and care and nurture their faith.

Matthew 18:10 states, *"See that you do not despise one of these little ones, for I say to you that their angels in Heaven continually see the face of My Father who is in Heaven."* Here, Jesus emphasizes the value and importance of children in the eyes of God. He urges His disciples, and by extension, all believers, to avoid despising or neglecting children. He highlights the divine connection between children and their heavenly guardians, emphasizing that their Angels have direct access to God's presence. This verse serves as a reminder that children hold a special place in God's heart and deserve our care and attention.

In Matthew 18:6, Jesus further emphasizes the significance of children's well-being and spiritual growth. He states,

"But whoever causes one of these little ones who believe in Me to stumble, it would be better for him to have a heavy millstone hung around his neck and to be drowned in the depths of the sea."

This powerful statement underscores the seriousness of influencing children negatively or leading them astray from their faith. Jesus highlights the severe consequences for those who hinder the spiritual journey of children who believe in Him. It serves as a warning against causing harm or being an obstacle to the faith development of young believers.

These verses demonstrate Jesus' deep concern for children and emphasize the responsibility we have as parents, caregivers, and members of society to protect, nurture, and support their spiritual growth. They remind us of the preciousness of children in God's sight and the importance of creating an environment that fosters their faith, ensuring they are not led astray or harmed in their journey with Christ.

Paul also said this in the Church of Ephesus:

"Fathers, do not provoke your children to anger, but bring them up in the discipline and instruction of the Lord." (Ephesians 6:4).

In all we know, children are one of the most precious beings in God's eyes. Jesus showed the significance of how important children are in the world. Now, why is this important? First, children believe in almost anything. You tell them to go pray for someone, and they will do it. You ask them to make something out of play dough; whatever they want, they will do. Suppose you tell them that Santa Claus is the one who delivers Christmas presents under the tree every Christmas morning. In that case, they will know that Santa loves cookies and milk because they heard it from their teachers or friends.

Do you see why, in the last sentence I just wrote, they listened to the stories of Santa from their teachers or friends and not from their parents? Do you remember what I talked about in earlier chapters—that it is encountering or influencing that produces our beliefs?

It's essential to see that our kids grow up with Godly lives. Kids are most joyful when young, so Jesus protects those who despise them. It's a sin to cause kids who believe in Him to stumble on their faith. Consider how great the consequences of your actions may be and how they can affect their lives.

And with doctrine, you have to establish a foundation where they know that God is good, even to help with the issues in their lives. They see the joy in Him and how He is pleased to have them. You must instruct and lovingly discipline them, not how your parents taught you. Exercise wisdom from what they taught you, but the best counselor is the Holy Spirit.

And so, to make a point, know how to love children the way Christ loves them. It's one thing to teach them how to cultivate the land, and it's another thing to steward the land with the Lord. In that, you can learn how to be a child in the faith. Be mature in your mind, but have a childlike faith in your heart and avoid evil.

"Brethren, do not be children in your thinking; yet in evil be infants, but in your thinking be mature." (1 Corinthians 14:20)

Rediscovering Purpose and Surrendering to God's Plan

Growing up, I always tried to figure out my life's purpose. I was proud never to be able to change or take a step. Before I dedicated my life to the Lord, I almost went to the Air Force to serve part-time and go full-time to college. I was very close to getting processed, and by the grace of God, He took me out by getting released by MEPS (Military Entrance Processing Station). Most of my family was against me going, and I didn't even care what they had to think. My goal was to become successful, and eventually, I knew at some point I was going to read my Bible while I was serving and attending my local community college. During COVID, I was almost at rock bottom as a whole. I broke my mom's heart many times, and it was tough because I used to hate seeing my mom cry. My mom is the reason why I carried purity and peace, and she had Jesus in her.

My mom has taken care of me so much, spoiled me with all the toys I had as a kid, been present at hospitals I had to go to when I had issues with my stomach, and many more. Yet, I continued to be disobedient to things I didn't want to do when told to do so. And even during COVID, when I tried to join the Air Force, my mom gave up on convincing me. *"You can do whatever you want."* As if I saw, she has lost hope in me. It broke my heart that I became so stoic about it. I became the old self that was stoic when I was a kid. I wasn't the only one who wanted to join the military. Many of my guy cousins had the same thought and were convinced by their parents to look for other options, and they did. Most end up having successful businesses in trucking and in the car industry.

Back then, I wasn't in the best shape, but one of the reasons I was letting go of the process was due to a condition called tachycardia. It's a condition where your average heart rate is above one hundred beats per minute. It was strange because my resting rate was usually around an average of 80, but I also took a Red Bull that same day. Drinking Red Bull wasn't wise to take before a medical exam in my worst shape. I took the Red

Bull because I woke up early at 3 a.m. at a hotel I was staying at in Seattle. I also had to take Melatonin before I went to bed to knock out to get much rest and then pop a Red Bull to start the day right. I even researched and studied carefully, knowing that depending on where I served in the Air Force, it would not be the best experience.

I asked friends who served in the military or are serving with all the information they had given me. Afterward, I gave up all the plans I had. My older brother convinced me after an hour of conversation in the car on the way back from Oregon to Washington after sharing what I wanted to do.

I decided to quit the idea of going to the military, submit to what my family called me to do, and start working in our family trucking business. Yet, I was still figuring out what to do, and just as I shared at the beginning of this book, I met the Lord once again.

Lessons from the Prodigal Son: Finding Redemption and Restoration

I felt lost most of my life, even when I didn't feel lost, because I couldn't care less and decided to figure out what to do or waste time on pointless things. And to compare my life, one of my favorite stories in the Bible that Jesus talked about is the Prodigal Son. This passage is exactly what I felt I went through similarly. A son who decided to take his father's inheritance and spend it all ate food with pigs. Here is the whole passage of the Prodigal Son; Jesus explained this story to the tax collectors and sinners:

"And He said, "A man had two sons. The younger of them said to his father, 'Father, give me the share of the estate that falls to me.' So, he divided his wealth between them. And not many days later, the younger son gathered everything together and went on a journey into a distant country, and there he squandered his estate with loose living. Now, when he had spent everything, a severe famine occurred in that country, and he began to be impoverished. So he went and hired himself out to one of the citizens of that country, and he sent him into his fields to feed swine. And he would have gladly filled his stomach with the pods that the swine were eating, and no one was giving anything to him. But when he came to his senses, he said, 'How many of my father's hired men have more than enough bread, but I am dying here with hunger!

I will get up and go to my father and will say to him, "Father, I have sinned against heaven, and in your sight, I am no longer worthy to be called your son; make me one of your hired men."' So he got up and came to his father. But while he was still a long way off, his father saw him, felt compassion for him, and ran and embraced him and kissed him. And the son said to him, 'Father, I have sinned against heaven and in your sight; I am no longer worthy to be called your son.' But the father said to his slaves, 'Quickly bring out the best robe and put it on him, and put a ring on his hand and sandals on his feet; and bring the fattened calf, kill it, and let us eat and celebrate; for this son of mine was dead and has come to life again; he was lost and has been found.' And they began to celebrate.

"Now his older son was in the field, and when he came and approached the house, he heard music and dancing. And he *summoned one of the servants and began inquiring about what these things could be. And he said to him, 'Your brother has come, and your father has killed the fattened calf because he has received him back safe and sound.' But he became angry and was not willing to go in, and his father came out and began pleading with him. But he answered and said to his father, 'Look! For so many years I have been serving you, and I have never neglected a command of yours; and yet you have never given me a young goat so that I might celebrate with my friends; but when this son of yours came, who has devoured your wealth with prostitutes, you killed the fattened calf for him.' And he said to him, 'Son, you have always been with me, and all that is mine is yours. But we had to celebrate and rejoice, for this brother of yours was dead, has begun to live, was lost, and has been found.'" (Luke 15:11–32 (NASB95)*

The perspective of the Father towards His children is profound and deeply moving. This passage evokes parallels with the story of Jacob and Esau, where Esau, driven by hunger, traded his birthright to Jacob for a simple bowl of stew, failing to consider the gravity of his actions. Within Jewish culture, this narrative carries the significance that the nation's existence is rooted in the mercy bestowed upon them.

The prodigal son, too, was fixated on his inheritance and the blessings of his father, ultimately disrespecting him by asserting his entitlement to them. It is a painful realization that, as children, we often abuse the gifts bestowed upon us by our parents. I, too, have been guilty of such transgressions. In my youth, I succumbed to the temptation of stealing my mother's debit cards to make in-game purchases on the app store. In doing so, I abused the inheritance my mother had graciously provided, thereby dishonoring her. God has prepared us for a place, and He is a gentleman who is willing to help us out in need. The prodigal father doesn't leave his home to be with his son in sin, but rather, he reminds the prodigal son that there is always a way back home.

As a young child, I failed to comprehend the depth of my wrongdoing. Greed had taken hold of me, becoming one of my most formidable obstacles. In high school, I engaged in deceitful activities such as scamming people on platforms like eBay, engaging in gambling, and other ill-intentioned pursuits. I was driven by a desire to acquire blessings and possess things that I did not rightfully deserve.

Reflecting on these actions, I now recognize the profound impact they had on my relationship with my parents and the harm I caused. It fills me with remorse and deep regret for the pain I inflicted upon them. I have come to understand the magnitude of their love and the sacrifices they made for my well-being.

These experiences serve as a humbling reminder of the importance of cherishing and respecting the blessings bestowed upon us by our parents. It is a call to abandon the path of greed and entitlement and embrace a mindset of gratitude and humility. May we learn from our past mistakes and strive to honor our parents, recognizing the immeasurable value of their love and provision.

The Father's Unconditional Love and Forgiveness (Kezazah)

As I delved into the entirety of this passage, I was astounded by the father's remarkable response to his wayward son. It struck me how, even within Jewish culture, the act of revealing one's legs, typically covered by robes, could be considered dishonorable. Yet, disregarding societal expectations, the father disregarded all decorum and ran towards his son, embracing and showering him with kisses. The significance of this act is not lost on me. Imagine that, with the length of his robe, he had to gather it up in order to run.

In Jewish tradition, there existed a practice known as "Kezazah," a ceremony where a large pot filled with manure, dirt, flowers, or fruits would be shattered in front of a son who had abandoned the culture. This symbolic act severed all ties and signified the son's complete disinheritance and abandonment by the community. It was a public declaration of shame, guilt, and condemnation. However, the prodigal father chose to spare his son from this humiliating ceremony. He ran to him, preventing the village from witnessing the son's disgrace and the consequential trouble that would follow. The moment the father locked eyes on his son, he didn't wait for repentance; he immediately showed love and forgiveness. He extended his forgiveness even before the son could seek it.

What astounds me further is the striking contrast between the two sons: one lost and then found, and the other faithfully working and honoring his father. The issue with the older brother in the passage lies in his jealousy and bitterness towards his father. Despite toiling for many years, he saw his father lavishing the returning son with a celebratory reception as if the prodigal son had made an extraordinary profit.

However, as the father stated, both sons held the same authority and inheritance. This passage highlights the father's generosity and equal love for both of his sons.

What captivates my attention is what the father gave the returning son when he decided to summon his servants to dress him. The father's actions demonstrate his desire to restore his son's dignity and honor. The son, who had squandered his inheritance and experienced utter destitution, was now adorned in the finest attire, signifying his reinstatement into the family and the restoration of his identity as a beloved son.

This intense story shows the transformative power of love, forgiveness, and restoration. It teaches us about the boundless grace and compassion that can be extended toward those who have strayed and the need to overcome jealousy and bitterness. The prodigal father's actions are a powerful reminder of the immense depth of a parent's love and the immeasurable worth each child holds in their eyes.

First, the father quickly called the servant with these three items in hand: "But the father said to his slaves, 'Quickly bring out the best robe and put it on him and put a ring on his hand and sandals on his feet;" (Luke 15:22). The robe represents the robe of righteousness. We become righteous with God. Isaiah said this to back up the prophecy in the new covenant.

"I will rejoice greatly in the Lord, My soul will exult in my God; For He has clothed me with garments of salvation, He has wrapped me with a robe of righteousness, As a bridegroom decks himself with a garland, And as a bride adorns herself with her jewels" (Isaiah 61:10).

And,

"For all of us have become like one who is unclean, And all our righteous deeds are like a filthy garment, And all of us wither like a leaf, And our iniquities, like the wind, take us away." (Isaiah 64:6).

The Bible verse that relates to the content is 2 Corinthians 5:17–19, which states:

"Therefore, if anyone is in Christ, the new creation has come: the old has gone, the new is here! All this is from God, who reconciled us to himself through Christ and gave us the ministry of reconciliation: that God was reconciling the world to himself in Christ, not counting people's sins against them. And he has committed to us the message of reconciliation."

This passage highlights the transformative power of being in Christ, where we become a new creation. It emphasizes that through Christ, God has reconciled us to Himself, and in His love and mercy, He does not hold our sins against us. Instead, He offers us the ministry of reconciliation, entrusting us with the message of His love and forgiveness. It underscores the significance of Jesus' sacrifice in bringing us closer to God and restoring our relationship with Him. How great is our father? Knowing that He is present when we run to Him.

The Path to Accessing the Father's Heart

The next item was the authority; the ring signifies that we have the same authority as the Father. In other words, whatever the Father did, so did Jesus in One with the Holy Spirit. And lastly, the sandals are one of the armor pieces God has given us in Ephesians with the gospel of peace (see Ephesians 6:15). We receive these items because Jesus died on our behalf so that we could access and have authority to do the Father's will and not our own. And this is the nature of the Father. He has given us the same access as people who are lost and come back or have been in ministry for years but felt like they didn't receive what they wanted from Him. There is no such thing as favoritism; God rewards those who diligently seek Him, regardless of what knowledge they carry but the knowledge of Christ. Paul was determined to know nothing except Jesus Christ and Him crucified (see 1 Corinthians 2:2).

We come up with many ideas and thoughts about how we approach the Father because of our circumstances and the sins we have committed in the past. Imagine the children who acknowledge that their parents are good parents who look out for their kids. Even to create a belief in them that as they grow up in adulthood, they make mistakes through disobedience, and it comes with severe consequences. This is why building relationships is important; you start to see who they are and how you can navigate your emotions through different relationships. For example, if I have a mentor who is wise and wants me to grow, then I will trust them with what I am facing.

Most importantly, to also teach people how easy it is to access the Father and receive Him in our hearts—letting Him comfort our hearts through our troubles. He is our Heavenly Father who wants to care for us, but we make it so complicated to approach Him. Why do we catch up with our feelings? We must take our successes, failures, personal desires, thoughts, and knowledge and submit them to God. The Romans say it like this:

"or if we live, we live for the Lord, or if we die, we die for the Lord; therefore, whether we live or die, we are the Lord's." (Romans 14:8).

No matter how our lives look, we are in the Lord. We don't have the right to follow our own paths when we belong to the Lord. He has rightfully owned us, but it's not that we are slaves to Him; rather, we are bond-servants as sons and daughters in the Kingdom of God. A bond servant is a slave who voluntarily serves the Lord, but the difference is that we aren't slaves or orphans. We are His friends. Jesus said this to His disciples in relation to each other.

"This is My commandment, that you love one another, just as I have loved you. Greater love has no one than this, that one laid down his life for his friends. You are My friends if you do what I command you. No longer do I call you slaves, for the slave does not know what his master is doing; but I have called you friends, for all things that I have heard from My Father I have made known to you. You did not choose Me but I chose you, and appointed you that you would go and bear fruit, and that your fruit would remain, so that whatever you ask of the Father in My name He may give to you. This I command you, that you love one another." (John 16:12-17)

We have access to and the right to the Father through the Son. If we say that salvation is a one-time thing we accept and do not continue walking in salvation, then we're not walking in the gospel. If we say that we are obedient to our parents yet still walk in disobedience throughout our day, then are we walking in obedience?

We walk in obedience and try to fill the issues in our hearts with music; for example, to calm or relate to it depends on our moods. Not to say that music is terrible, but where are you pouring your issues? And what's worse is not bringing your problems to light.

Your life is meant to break. Be open to the people around you who walk like Jesus so that you can be filled with grace and compassion. We cannot comprehend what kind of relationship Jesus and the Father had. Yet, they are both one God, including the Holy Spirit. It was, in essence, raw, authentic, and vulnerable in many ways possible. Being raw with the Father is how He shows His heart to you; you must be blind to see that it's impossible; He wouldn't. Righteousness brings relationships, but you cannot have righteousness without salvation. You can't have salvation without grace, and you can't have grace without faith.

The Church needs to wake up and see that if they aren't experiencing the fullness of God, just as I mentioned many times in this book, then we are blind to seeing Him rightly.

"For by grace you have been saved through faith; and that not of yourselves, it is the gift of God; not as a result of works, so that no one may boast. For we are His workmanship, created in Christ Jesus for good works, which God prepared beforehand so that we would walk in them." (Ephesians 2:8-10)

The Redemptive Sacrifice and Fatherly Love

God is a good Father, no matter how you see it. He isn't an old man with a long white beard who shakes his fist at us every time we sin. Many people haven't seen that yet because of fear. Fear is a dangerous root to carry, so we allow God to prune and change the root in our hearts. Fear is what disables us from achieving anything in life. The fear of stepping out, the fear of man, thinking about what others think, et cetera. Suppose we continue to believe that our view of the Father is punishing. What are we doing if we continue to walk in condemnation? The belief of feeling disapproved by the Father when He came in the flesh to die for our condemnation?

The Father is looking for those willing to open their hearts to Him, and He pours out His heart so we can become more like Him. Abraham put His faith in God, and the Father made him righteous. The difficulty was how far Abraham's obedience was to go before he was called to sacrifice Isaac, his son. God blessed and established a covenant with Abraham as a father of many nations (see Genesis 17:1–7). Of course, in the old covenant, sacrifices were needed to please God and temporarily cover a person's sins. More so, it was God who tested Abraham's faith and did not intend to allow Abraham to sacrifice Isaac. What was so interesting about the story of Abraham and Isaac was that Abraham was the Father of many nations. And in the story, Moses wrote this in Genesis:

"Then they came to the place of which God had told him, and Abraham built the altar there, arranged the wood, bound his son Isaac, and laid him on the altar, on top of the wood. Abraham stretched out his hand and took the knife to slay his son. But the angel of the Lord called to him from heaven and

said, "Abraham, Abraham!" And he said, "Here I am." He said, "Do not stretch out your hand against the lad, and do nothing to him; for now I know that you fear God since you have not withheld your son, your only son, from Me." (Genesis 22:9-12).

The final verse of this passage reflects on the angel of the Lord's statement about Abraham not withholding his only son, Isaac, from God. Symbolically, Abraham represents God the Father, while Isaac represents Jesus, even down to the altar being built with wood.

The sacrifice of Isaac foreshadowed the ultimate sacrifice of Christ, who willingly carried His cross. God sent His Son, Jesus, to redeem the sins of the world. One might question why God would allow Jesus to suffer and be crucified, questioning if it was an act of abuse.

However, it was a mutual agreement between the Father and the Son to bring about redemption. Jesus fully obeyed the Father, understanding He would endure suffering on the cross. He lived a perfect life without disobedience or sin. By His own free will, Jesus chose to go to the cross, providing hope for humanity. Without this act, there would be no atonement for sins, and the prophecies in the Old Testament, including those in the book of Isaiah, would be meaningless.

The entirety of Scripture points to Jesus and God's plan for us to walk in righteousness. As human beings, we cannot question God's decisions and wish for things to be different. We do not possess the knowledge and understanding to compare with God's divine purpose. If we choose to believe in another way, we will perceive God as weak, strange, or incapable of answering our difficult questions. Jesus, who is righteous and died on our behalf, grants us access to that same righteousness when we believe in Him.

We are encouraged to reflect on our own lives and acknowledge where we have fallen short. The essence of the Gospel is about the intimate relationship between God and humanity, not about theological debates or comparing one's knowledge of God. The central truth remains that God loved the world so much that He sent His Son to die for us, providing redemption, reconciliation, justification, sanctification, and salvation. Through faith in Jesus, we can stand as righteous sons and daughters in the Kingdom of God.

We build the basis for a path toward righteousness and reconciliation with God by putting our confidence in Him. Second, we must submit our lives to God and accept His standard of rule because of His love for us. We must acknowledge that we are not in control and that God's ways are beyond our comprehension. When we surrender to His will, we allow His transformational power to work on us. It necessitates humility, letting go of our ambitions, and striving to match our lives with God's plan.

Also, comprehending the breadth of God's love is critical. As a show of great love for humanity, He sent His Son, Jesus. Recognizing this fact inspires thankfulness and a desire to live in accordance with His teachings. We may deepen our awareness of God's love and allow it to affect our lives by immersing ourselves in the Scriptures and cultivating a personal connection with Him.

Furthermore, actively living out the solution involves embracing the ministry of reconciliation. Just as God reconciled us to Himself through Christ, we are called to be ambassadors of reconciliation in the world. It means showing forgiveness, love, and compassion to others. By sharing the message of God's redeeming grace and participating in acts of reconciliation, we become agents of positive change, reflecting God's love and righteousness.

Chapter 7: The Mindset

Renewing the Mind: Breaking Free from Negative Thought Patterns

Every day, we have a constant battle in our minds. I discussed the mind many times in this book, but our mind always catches up with something. We can only control a tiny part of our conscious mind. The majority of thinking comes from subconscious mindsets. Your mind immediately doesn't categorize the incoming thoughts as essential; instead, wait and monitor how you treat that thought. In this chapter, I want to touch on how we can renew our minds throughout our Christian lives. Self-control is one of the fruits we must bear from the Holy Spirit.

The mind is often understood as a faculty that manifests in mental phenomena like reasoning, thinking, belief, desire, emotion, and motivation. The mind doesn't mean your brain; it is instead the real you inside. How do your thoughts play through the day? Thoughts can be played repeatedly as tapes, and sometimes, it's challenging to get rid of the evil thoughts in our minds. Neurons are information messengers that send out electrical impulses to send information to different areas of your brain and your nervous system. What we transmit is based on how we encounter and experience the past. Some may have gone through trauma and could never get rid of it.

The right side of the brain plays a part when it is involved in creative thinking by simply relaxing. At the same time, the left side of the brain plays a part in logical and analytical thinking.

Often, it's mistaken by the devil, and the more we continue to blame the devil, the probability that we may blame God for why we can't get rid of this evil thought in our minds. It isn't the issue of the devil, but it's something we allow the devil to carry. By free will, we can hold fast to what is good or bad. The Father allows mature sons to have what they want or have in their lives. As I talked about the prodigal son in the last chapter, consider how the story of the prodigal father didn't stop the younger son from leaving with his inheritance. The father wasn't controlling, loved his son, and was aware of how responsible his son may be.

The Garden of Eden: Unveiling Deception and Disobedience in the Mind

If you think about the Garden of Eden, God allowed Adam and Eve to do what they wanted, and He warned the two not to eat the fruit of knowledge and evil. God entrusted them, and through Eve's deception, sin came in because the simple rule was to not eat the fruit. God could have intervened and prevented the most significant catastrophe from slipping into humanity. It's not God's intention for the fall of man to happen, but He allowed free will so we could choose Him. If He did intervene, it would not be love. Love does not look like forcing someone. For example, if we were to be on social media all day, he wouldn't come in and shut off your phone to spend time with Him. He's a gentleman, and until you put down your phone and seek Him, that's when you start to see Him rightly. When we can look at Him and see Him rightly in His presence, we start to see what His love looks like according to the Word. He still loves us despite what we have done; but He wants to guide us into laying down the desires of the flesh. And so, with a mind that explores and becomes curious. When do we know what is right according to the law of morality? We're taught that it isn't right to go there, and yet we go there.

It wasn't that Eve had an evil thought of eating the fruit, but she was deceived into thinking it was right. Somebody can say a fact about one thing you heard for years and find out it's all been a lie. Adam and Eve were innocent people. The enemy used deception as the best way to cause the two to fall. Why does the Church believe disobedience to God caused them to sin? It's part of it, yes, because they weren't supposed to eat the fruit, but it's another way that deception can look right and innocent until we find out it was a lie. A lie is something that contradicts the truth, but deception is believing in the lie as the truth. Suppose their union with God was so perfect that even we could never reach that level of intimacy. How can evil enter their minds? Even so, there was no knowledge of good or evil to begin with. It was pure, innocent, holy, spotless, and blameless.

They can't turn away from God except through deception because the Lord firmly holds their spirit. Their hearts could never fall away from God. If only Eve had the awareness and revelation to remain obedient to God. The issue, I believe, is that she lacked understanding of the Father because she came second after Adam, and Adam spent more time with the Lord.

Now, scripturally, this interaction that I will share is in Scripture. We don't have an exact interaction between Adam and Eve, just like we don't have an entire description of Jesus' life other than when He was born in the world, then when He was 12 years old, and His life between the ages of 30-33 years. We don't know what exactly went down in Jesus' life on Earth other than His motives for humanity, including how He's literally gone from Genesis to Revelation. He is the Word, and there's more than we ought to think about in terms of His nature and His likeness, according to the scriptures. I believe how Adam reacted to Eve, knowing that she had eaten the fruit and would have been kicked out of the garden due to disobedience. Considering that once she has left the Garden, Adam will be alone, although he had God with Him, it wasn't God's plan to separate the two from each other. However, God would have to protect the Tree of Life from Eve to inherit eternal life with a sinful conscience. Therefore, Adam did not want to be alone, and scripture says Eve was only deceived while Adam ate the fruit by free will. Let's look at Genesis and see what the passage says after they have eaten the fruit.

"They heard the sound of the Lord God walking in the garden in the cool of the day, and the man and his wife hid themselves from the presence of the Lord God among the trees of the garden. Then the Lord God called to the man and said to him, "Where are you?" He said, "I heard the sound of You in the garden, and I was afraid because I was naked, so I hid myself." And He said, "Who told you that you were naked? Have you eaten from the tree of which I commanded you not to eat?" The man said, "The woman whom You gave to be with me, she gave me from the tree, and I ate." Then the Lord God said to the woman, "What is this you have done?" And the woman said, "The serpent deceived me, and I ate." (Genesis 3:8-13).

Before this incident, the serpent had deceived Eve by assuring her that death would not be a consequence of acquiring the knowledge of good and evil. The passage doesn't specifically describe how the interaction between Eve and Adam took place when she passed him the fruit. However, it is believed that Adam's relationship with God was so perfect that he willingly chose to partake in sin in order to be with Eve. It parallels the sacrifice of Christ on the cross, where he willingly took upon himself the burden of our sins to be with us.

The Distortion of Adam's Mind: Unveiling Shame, Guilt, and Condemnation

Adam's mind was filled with distortion, even though he possessed intellect and consciousness. Blaming Eve for succumbing to the temptation of eating the forbidden fruit, Adam fails to recognize the true source of his distorted thoughts. When God confronted them, questioning why they were afraid and hiding, as well as why they believed themselves to be naked, He sought to expose the deception that had clouded their perception. God's response, *"Who told you that you were naked?"* uncovered the lie that had been cunningly planted by the enemy to manipulate and distort their sense of self.

This pivotal moment marked a profound shift in Adam and Eve's perception of themselves and their relationship with God. The opening of their eyes to their newfound vulnerability evoked three distinct emotions within them, each contributing to their overall sense of disorientation and separation.

Firstly, shame engulfed their beings, manifesting as a pervasive feeling of being inherently wrong and unworthy. Their nakedness, once innocently embraced, now became a symbol of their perceived imperfection and inadequacy. The shame they experienced was a direct result of their awareness of their own vulnerability and the consequences of their disobedience. Accompanying shame was an overwhelming sense of guilt. They recognized that their actions had been morally wrong, and an indelible regret began to take root within them. The weight of their transgression bore heavily upon their souls as they yearned for a return to the innocence and obedience they had lost.

Moreover, condemnation became a prevailing belief in their hearts. They started to view God as an angry and disapproving figure, convinced that He would judge and reject them for their disobedience. This perception of God's disapproval fueled their desire to distance themselves from Him, leading them to retreat and hide. Adam and Eve's emotional turmoil, comprising shame, guilt, and condemnation, stemmed from their distorted understanding of their own identity and their strained relationship with God. The enemy's deceit had successfully manipulated their perception, obscuring the truth of their inherent worth and the unconditional love of their Creator.

Adam's mind became utterly different after he loved God and Eve as himself. It went from being intimate with the two to separation. And that the cause of separations was confusion. Adam was confused because of the manipulation of lies. The lies that came upon Adam's identity and that identity in Him were ruined. It can never be fixed until God finally sends His son first to fulfill every Law he has given to His people and takes sin upon himself when others inflict Jesus. To get right with Father and come back to the garden.

In the book of Genesis, we witness the devastating consequences of sin entering the world and corrupting not only the hearts and minds of humanity but also the very fabric of creation itself. However, the redemptive work of Jesus Christ offers a glimmer of hope amidst this corruption. Through His sacrificial act, Jesus willingly bore the weight of the crown of thorns upon His mind, signifying the extent to which He suffered to bring us peace and restore our soundness of mind.

A powerful biblical verse, 2 Timothy 1:7, sheds light on the transformative nature of God's intervention in our minds. In some translations, it states that God has bestowed upon us a *spirit of power, love, and a sound mind.* This verse, such as in the New King James Version (NKJV), highlights the importance of having a sound and disciplined mind, guided by the Holy Spirit's power and infused with love.

When our minds are transformed by the indwelling presence of the Holy Spirit, we gain the ability to hold fast to the truths that God speaks about us. Our thoughts and perspectives align with His divine wisdom and promises. This transformation allows us to overcome the corruption and distortions that sin has wrought within our minds, enabling us to live in accordance with God's purpose and plan for our lives.

God's desire is to restore the right mindset to those who are lost or trapped in the clutches of mental corruption. He longs to bring healing and clarity to the brokenness within our thoughts and emotions. Through the redemptive work of Jesus Christ and the empowering presence of the Holy Spirit, we can experience a renewed and sound mind, free from the chains of sin and corruption.

As we yield ourselves to God's transformative power, embracing the spirit of power, love, and a sound mind, we open ourselves to His restoration and guidance. He replaces confusion with clarity, despair with hope, and turmoil with peace. Our renewed mindset enables us to navigate life's challenges with discernment and wisdom emanating from the wellspring of God's truth and love within us.

Unveiling the Power of the Mind: From False Identities to Righteous Morality

The mind encompasses more than just the physical brain; it resides in the space between the intellect and the heart. How we cultivate our relationship with the Lord directly impacts our transformation into His likeness. In His divine wisdom, God rewards those who diligently seek Him in hidden places, away from the public eye. However, the secret place is not a physical location like a private room or a secluded area; rather, it exists within the depths of our minds. It is the intimate space where our true selves reside, away from the masks we wear to conceal false identities.

False identity is a burden many of us carry, causing us to react with intense distress when our buttons are pushed. It may manifest as a secret we are too ashamed to share, an issue we are embarrassed to confront, or the deep-seated pain of past abuse, fearing how others might respond. Moreover, there are those who speak falsehoods into the identities of others, perpetuating harmful misconceptions and stereotypes. Consider the example of a young boy growing up without a father figure, raised solely by a nurturing mother. Society may draw assumptions about his behavior, assuming femininity equates to homosexuality, due to the lack of true fatherhood.

This misguided labeling plants seeds of doubt and confusion within the boy's mind, causing him to question his own identity and wrestle with his understanding of sexuality. The way he approaches and internalizes these thoughts may have deep and lasting effects on his life. A single decision, influenced by societal expectations and personal struggles, can set the course for his entire existence, potentially leading to a chain reaction of sin and its consequences. This principle applies to any moral judgment, as our choices define and shape our sense of self. It is through these experiences, trials, and soul-searching that we grapple with our understanding of what is right and wrong, constantly testing and questioning our beliefs.

It is important to recognize that we were never intended to possess knowledge of good and evil apart from God. He alone holds that divine wisdom. Yet, we find ourselves unintentionally or intentionally making poor choices in life, succumbing to the allure of sin, and straying from God's intended path for us. Our human nature is flawed and prone to error. However, it is through our relationship with God, seeking His guidance, and surrendering to His transformative power that we can navigate the complexities of our minds and find redemption and restoration.

The mind is a complex and delicate entity intertwined with our intellect, emotions, and spiritual essence. It is in this realm that our true selves are revealed, where false identities must be dismantled and replaced with the truth of who God created us to be. By aligning our thoughts and choices with His divine wisdom, we can overcome the struggles of false identity, make sound decisions, and find our ultimate purpose and fulfillment in Him.

The concept of the law of morality is one of my favorite things that C.S. Lewis has talked about in his book, *'Mere Christianity.'* To my knowledge, it is our instincts we call good in our minds. It also stops you from having a good time by looking at the joy it offers because we tend to believe in what is *good* in our lives. In reality, moral rules are directions for running the human machine.[1] God has written the laws so that we can have morality. The Bible verse from the book of Jeremiah, as quoted in Hebrews 10:15-17, serves as a powerful testament to the transformative work of the Holy Spirit within believers. It states,

"And the Holy Spirit also testifies to us; for after saying, 'This is the covenant that I will make with them after those days, says the Lord: I will put My laws upon their hearts, and on their minds I will write them,' He then says, 'And their sins and their lawless deeds I will remember no more.'"

This verse highlights the promise of a new covenant established by God. In the Old Testament, God's laws were external, written on stone tablets, and delivered through the Mosaic Law. However, through the work of Jesus Christ and the

---

[1]Lewis, C.S. Mere Christianity. Geoffrey Bles, 1952. p. 69.

indwelling of the Holy Spirit, God's laws are now inscribed upon the hearts and minds of His people. This internal transformation enables believers to align their thoughts, desires, and actions with God's divine principles.

The verse from Jeremiah, referenced in Hebrews, emphasizes God's desire to establish a more intimate connection with His people. The external observance of the law was not sufficient to bring about true righteousness and forgiveness of sins. Therefore, God initiated a new covenant, one that would involve a profound inner transformation through the power of the Holy Spirit. In this new covenant, God's grace replaces the need for continual sacrifices and offerings to atone for sin.

The recognition of morality and the distinction between right and wrong, even among non-believers, reflect the innate sense of God's moral law written upon their hearts. This universal understanding points to the existence of a higher standard of righteousness that transcends cultural and societal norms. The corruption and wickedness observed in the world evoke a reaction because, deep down, people have a sense of what is morally wrong.

In the Old Testament, the extent of corruption became so pervasive that God chose to bring judgment upon the earth through the great flood during the time of Noah (Genesis 6). This was done so that humanity would not be filled with evil but with new hope. God is not just a judge who declares innocent or guilty, but one who delivers people. Similarly, Moses was a man used by God to deliver the Israelites out of slavery in Egypt. Later on, the giving of the Mosaic Law to Moses marked a significant turning point in God's interaction with humanity. The Law served as a guide for righteous living, revealing God's standards and outlining the consequences of disobedience.

Yet, the old covenant, based on the Levitical priesthood and animal sacrifices, was not the ultimate solution for the complete forgiveness of sins. God had a greater plan in mind. Through Jesus Christ, the new covenant was established, offering a way for humanity to be reconciled with God. By wholeheartedly following and surrendering to Jesus, believers are empowered by the Holy Spirit to live according to God's commands and experience His transforming grace.

As believers devote their minds, souls, and strength to God, aligning their lives with His teachings, they enter into a state of righteousness and right standing with Him. It is through this intimate relationship and the work of the Holy Spirit that believers are enabled to fulfill the requirements of the law and experience God's merciful forgiveness. The new covenant, rooted in the grace and love of God, provides the means for believers to live in accordance with His moral standards and experience true transformation. Not only that, but a lot of the old external Laws were done away.

Now, do we say we're sinless? Not necessarily; we sin less and less without the intention of sinning again. It's a part of sanctification. But we are dead to sin because of the finished work of the cross. The blood of Jesus washes our minds. Scientists say that our brains can carry three million years of information, and our brain has eighty-six billion neurons[2]. Yet,

---

[2]Houzel, Suzana H. "The Remarkable, yet Not Extraordinary, Human Brain As a Scaled-up Primate Brain and Its Associated Cost." PNAS, 22 Jun. 2012.

we can only use 3-4% of our brain daily. We start to learn from our mistakes and wrongdoing into doing what is right.

Renewing Your Mind: Embracing God's Design and Disciplined Transformation

Now, renewing your mind is another thing. The Bible doesn't talk too much about renewing your mind, but Scripture clearly says we are not to conform to the world. The renewal of your mind shapes the character God has designed you to be. God doesn't want people to walk with masks, but to change the person in righteousness. Your nature gets sanctified every day. Of course, it will change, but how good is it that your personality becomes Godly? Reading your Bible is the best way God can speak to you, as well as speak through many things.

Our minds will always collect new information daily, and the information we receive can lead us somewhere, whether good or bad. Be careful how your mind flows. God renews your mind, and the people He sends you will be drawn to Him. It is the blood of Jesus that draws you near to Him. The blood of Jesus has washed your mind, and if you hold fast to what the Word of God says, you will be drawn and renewed. The mind of Christ and the heart of Jesus surpass all knowledge and understanding. God's wisdom is far greater than man's wisdom. He is more significant than us. He is God who understands it all.

The gospel isn't to only believe once, and that's it. You continue believing in Him daily; He will draw you near to Him. Knowing you deal with sin, He can wash it clean and clear your mind of evil consciousness. It's to recognize that once you are born again and seek Him, you will never want to return to your old mindset. It's a matter of where you put your mind. The Holy Spirit is what draws you to the Son. To grow, you give your life to Christ, not a one-time experience. A man who walks double-mindedly will not see the fruit of His life in Christ.

"But if any of you lacks wisdom, let him ask of God, who gives to all generously and without reproach, and it will be given to him. But he must ask in faith without any doubt, for the one who doubts is like the surf of the sea, driven and tossed by the wind. For that man ought not to expect that he will receive anything from the Lord, being a double-minded man, unstable in all his ways." (James 1:5-8)

And,

"Therefore, brethren, since we have confidence to enter the holy place by the blood of Jesus, by a new and living way which He inaugurated for us through the veil, that is, His flesh, and since we have a great priest over the house of God, let us draw near with a sincere heart in full assurance of faith, having our hearts sprinkled clean from an evil conscience and our bodies washed with pure water. Let us hold fast the confession of our hope without wavering, for He who promised is faithful; and let us consider how to stimulate one another to love and good deeds, not forsaking our own assembling together, as is the habit of some, but encouraging one another; and all the more as you see the day drawing near." (Hebrews 11:19-25)

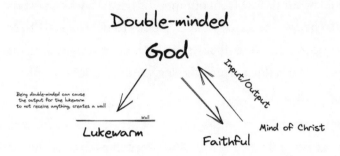

Discipline is one other way to renew your mind. I knew that when I returned with the Lord in 2021, I wanted the Lord to change me. I didn't care what my dignity looked like because I gave myself to Him every day. My mind is now filled with Godly thoughts. It isn't because I just read my Bible. I read *and meditate* on scripture every day. Meditation is biblical, according to Joshua, who says this:

"This book of the law shall not depart from your mouth, but you shall meditate on it day and night, so that you may be careful to do according to all that is written in it; for then you will make your way prosperous, and then you will have success.'" (Joshua 1:8).

The Power of the Mind: Embracing Truth, Renewing Identity

Not only do you believe in God's Word, but you also have to act upon it in your life. You have to make the Word real to you, and it truly does give life. Reading the Word without the Spirit is like reading the Law, a set of rules and dos and don'ts. When we look at a verse that the Holy Spirit draws us to, we meditate on it to recite it in our minds. Joshua says that the book of the law should never depart from our mouths because when we preach, talk to people, or share what God does to us. You start to speak life into others. The Bible says that what comes out of our innermost will flows rivers of living water (see John 7:38).

You start to speak into people's lives by allowing and opening your heart to the Lord so that He can speak through you as an individual. The Word becomes heart knowledge instead of head knowledge. And in that way, your spiritual wealth, which I can call storage, God stores His nature in you so that you can be prosperous. Your mind is so important; we can't let the enemy do what he pleases. God has given us the mind of Christ to have the authority to rebuke evil. Jesus even said that the Holy Spirit is what draws us to the truth:

"I have many more things to say to you, but you cannot bear them now. But when He, the Spirit of truth, comes, He will guide you into all the truth; for He will not speak on His own initiative, but whatever He hears, He will speak; and He will disclose to you what is to come. He will glorify Me, for He will take of Mine and will disclose it to you. All things that the Father has are Mine; therefore, I said that He takes of Mine and will disclose it to you." (John 16:12-15).

We want to seek the truth in our lives. We want to find what denomination fits us, what drug can satisfy us, or what pleasure can do. We call these things *"truth."* to fulfill the purpose of our lives. We're so broken, never find the truth in our lives. When we allow the Holy Spirit to work in our hearts, we will find the truth God says is true. The Holy Spirit teaches us who Jesus is. The Holy Spirit draws us to the truth—our minds continually seek what kind of Jesus He is. And it is the best part. It is all based on your relationship with Him. God is not a god of religion; He is a God of relationships who wants to be with us and help us in this world.

The power of the gospel is to remind you that He is more than enough to reign over your life and to continue to triumph over you with humility. He has taken everything from this world so that it dies in the grave where He was buried. The thing that weighs you down. He rose again because God and the power of the Holy Spirit went into Him. After all, He fulfilled every law. He was tempted in all things and won. And now, He is sitting on the right hand of the Father, and through Him, we too can become righteous. God is victorious and wants every believer to reach the lost and reveal the Gospel's truth. You can't shape your identity without knowledge and understanding.

Unleashing the Power of the Gospel: Embracing the Mind of Christ

I want the Church to see what the Gospel can offer. We get so stuck up by so many things that we lose focus on the Gospel. It doesn't mean that the growth of Christianity is getting worse, but it's growing more and more in victory. But for some, I want people to understand that God is the true source of everything. And Paul reminds the Corinth Church how important it is to hold fast to His word.

"Now I make known to you, brethren, the Gospel which I preached to you, which also you received, in which also you stand, by which also you are saved if you hold fast the word which I preached to you unless you believed in vain. For I delivered to you as of first importance what I also received, that

Christ died for our sins according to the Scriptures, that He was buried, and that He was raised on the third day according to the Scriptures" (1 Corinthians 15:1-4).

You have received Him and are saved, but are you still struggling in sin? Consider the blood of Jesus. If He conquered the power of sin by taking Himself on the cross, what makes you think your sin is too powerful or unworthy for the blood to cover? I speak to those who may have struggled in sin. The gospel is never to be underestimated. It is beyond our comprehension that we can never fully understand the gospel. But we renew our minds by seeking Him every day. It is so worth it when you entirely lay down everything your mind has. Remember Him. To conclude this chapter, consider Peter's words:

"Therefore, prepare your minds for action, keep sober in spirit, and fix your hope completely on the grace to be brought to you at the revelation of Jesus Christ." (1 Peter 1:13)

Peter says to move forward in life with action. Completely fix your hope in Jesus in everything in your life. Christ is the finisher. It is the rest that comes from the finished work of the cross! You have the mind of Christ! With the mind of Christ, you understand who He is, and only believers can have access to that.

Chapter 8: Union in the Body

Unity: The Call for Unity and the Dangers of Vanity

Unity may well be one of the least talked about subjects in the Church. We know that unity means being united or joined as a whole. I sometimes ponder why it's not talked about in the Church. Is the subject hard to preach? Have we become selfish and focused on our lives rather than the lives of others? In noun form, Solomon said *'Vanity'* in the book of Ecclesiastes. Vanity is to say that a pastor has everything they need and does not look forward to what's next for their ministry. We have admired our work but not looked at the finished work—the author of our faith. We look at ourselves, and we seek glory from others in our admiration. "*Vanity, vanity, vanity,*" says Solomon. We look at things naturally in our eyes that are more pleasing than the Lord.

"For those who are according to the flesh set their minds on the things of the flesh, but those who are according to the Spirit, the things of the Spirit." (Romans 8:5)

"Therefore, I, the prisoner of the Lord, implore you to walk in a manner worthy of the calling with which you have been called, with all humility and gentleness, with patience, showing tolerance for one another in love, and being diligent to preserve the unity of the Spirit in the bond of peace. There is one body and one Spirit, just as you were called in one hope of your calling; one Lord, one faith, one baptism, one God, and one Father of all who is over all, through all, and in all." (Ephesians 4:1-6)

There is a terrible impulse to believe that the achievements we have made or how long we've grown in ministry are the work that got us there. In all things, the finished work produces rest in our lives. It is faith that produces works. Work is the fruit that builds in our lives. The deeds of the flesh come with many sinful behaviors, but the fruit comes from the finished work. I am repeating this because, in ministry or throughout our lives, we sometimes forget the finished work of the cross.

We must always remember what He's done and has done in our lives. It is not that we work, but He did it. And in one mind, heart, and body, we unite to help one another. Without unity, we would have never had the blessed world that we have today. Our skills, communication, and talents help create this world. God has blessed Adam to take care of the land. Therefore, humanity must tend the land, and we did it well. The technology, the cars, and the buildings are all united. How can one man do it all himself? Of course, God, the creator of all things, did it Himself—the creator of the heavens and earth. As humans, however, we're so limited in our understanding, yet we can learn more.

Our human limitations are a result of our finite nature compared to the infinite nature of God. Even Jesus, when He took on flesh, experienced limitations in His earthly ministry. There were times when He couldn't physically reach all the people in need, highlighting the concept of limitation. While we may understand how to serve others, we are limited in our ability to do so effectively on our own.

Jesus, despite being the chosen one and, for some, God Himself, chose to take on the form of a man and rely on the support of His disciples. It is evident in the account of the Mount of Olives, found in Luke 22:39–46. During this significant moment, Jesus was overwhelmed with the weight of what lay ahead. He shared a vision of His impending crucifixion, and the stress was so intense that He began to bleed from within, a condition known as hematidrosis (see Luke 22:44).

Jesus, in His humanity, sought solace and strength through prayer. He called His disciples to join Him and asked them to pray, specifically to avoid falling into temptation. He distanced Himself from them, going a short distance away, and kneeled down to pray. In His prayer, Jesus expressed His desire for the cup of suffering to be removed but ultimately submitted to the Father's will, saying, *"Yet not My will, but Yours be done."*

In that critical moment, an angel from heaven appeared to Jesus, strengthening Him. Despite the agony He was experiencing, Jesus fervently prayed. His sweat became like drops of blood, a powerful testimony to the intensity of His struggle. When He returned to His disciples, He found them sleeping, overcome with sorrow. He admonished them, urging them to wake up and pray to avoid temptation.

Jesus, in this vulnerable moment, demonstrated humility by relying on His disciples for support and intercession. He knew the weight of the cross He would bear and sought strength to fulfill His mission. It was in the garden of Gethsemane that Jesus confronted His most challenging and agonizing moment, as His soul was overwhelmed to the point of death. In His humility, He approached the Father, asking if there was any other way but ultimately surrendering to God's plan.

This passage from Luke 22:39–46 reveals Jesus's deep dependence on His disciples and His willingness to share His burden with them. It also serves as a reminder of Jesus's immense sacrifice and the tremendous weight He bore in order to accomplish the redemption of humanity. Jesus's humble plea to the Father exemplifies His commitment to fulfilling God's will, even in the face of overwhelming suffering.

The account of Jesus's prayer in the garden of Gethsemane underscores the limitations of our human nature and the importance of seeking support and strength from God and others.

Jesus's vulnerability and reliance on His disciples serve as an example for us to acknowledge our own limitations and seek assistance, both from God and from fellow believers. Through humility and dependence on God's will, we can navigate the challenges and burdens of life, just as Jesus did in His most trying hour. We need to have this kind of humility to seek community to build unity so that we don't fall into temptations. Isolation from others is a form of pride.

A Glimpse of Unity: Lessons from a Mission Trip to India and Brazil

On March 2, 2023, I embarked on a mission trip to India, which turned out to be one of the most extraordinary experiences of my life. Throughout our seventeen-day journey, my team and I had the privilege of witnessing numerous signs and wonders in the various locations we visited. However, it was during the first half of our trip, when we explored the southern part of India known as Eluru, that I encountered an incredibly impactful moment.

In Eluru, I was deeply moved by the remarkable level of honor that permeated Indian culture. The Christians I encountered displayed genuine servant hearts and held a profound reverence for the Lord. This level of faithfulness was something I rarely observed in my own country, the United States. It was astonishing to witness this unwavering devotion despite the challenging circumstances that many in India face, living in one of the world's less privileged regions.

The faithful hearts of Indian Christians served as a stark reminder of how grateful I am to live in one of the most secure countries on earth. It was a humbling realization that we often find ourselves complaining about trivial matters amid our abundance. I'm sure many of us can relate to this tendency in our own lives.

One of the striking aspects of the Indian Christians I encountered was their strong sense of unity. Some engaged in corporate study of the Word of God, while others sought His presence or displayed a deep passion for worship. My heart was stirred as I witnessed their devotion. Even the family with whom we stayed for a week exemplified this unity. Not only did they serve us food at the table, but they also went above and beyond by frequently offering to add more food to our plates.

Now, you might be thinking, *"Well, my family does that all the time."* That's wonderful! Keep up the good work! But when was the last time you saw someone *intentionally* caring for those around them? The hospitality we experienced in India was something entirely different from what we typically encounter. Their actions exuded the heart of the Father, demonstrating a love and care that is sadly rare in today's world.

Loving and caring for others is one of the most challenging things to do, yet Jesus commanded us to love our neighbors as ourselves. In the book I mentioned earlier, I explored how saying *"I love you"* after partnering with the Holy Spirit can make a significant difference. It's a powerful reminder that genuine love and compassion flow from a heart connected to the source of all love. In the book of 1 John, it says this:

"Little children, let us not love with word or with tongue, but in deed and truth." (1 John 3:18)

My mission trip to India opened my eyes to the beauty of a culture that values honor, displays unity, and practices selfless love. It reminded me of the importance of living with gratitude and intentionally caring for those around me. The experience left an indelible mark on my heart and deepened my understanding of what it means to follow Jesus with sincerity and devotion.

Similarly to Brazil, a trip I just recently went on back in March 2024 during my second year of ministry school at Kingdom Movement School of Ministry. I'm adding this story to my manuscript as well because what I've learned from my leader is that the most spiritual thing you can do on a mission trip is naturally build relationships with people. I was partnered with a missions base called 'Iris Fortaleza' and although it was only a week, the biggest takeaway for me was learning how to shepherd my team and my friends. As you read this book, you probably noticed the emphasis on who we are (which is what I want to aim for), but another thing is that I love to teach what is true. However, I do believe that a great teacher is a great student who asks questions that can open someone's heart. And just like my first missions trip in India, I can say that there was also a level of honor and unity, and the most important core value in the Brazil trip was: 'family.' The most spiritual thing you can do as a Christian is to spend time with your family.

And I think, as a body, we may have missed it. We missed the touch of unity in the Church. Where have the intentions we say we would take on but never come to pass? I'm talking more about relationships with people. I haven't seen anyone be as intentional in India (and now in Brazil) as in the United States. You know, we have been given the mind of Christ, but we are not acknowledging our gift of righteousness. In the book of Acts, there is a passage that immediately follows Peter's sermon on the Day of Pentecost, and it serves as a remarkable example of the early Church. This passage, found in Acts 2:43–47, illustrates the unity and selflessness that characterized the believers at that time.

The passage begins by describing how a sense of awe and wonder filled the people as they witnessed the apostles performing many signs and wonders through the power of the Holy Spirit. This supernatural manifestation reinforced the Gospel's message and drew people closer to God.

What follows is a demonstration of the believers' deep commitment to one another. They were united in their faith and shared a common purpose. They sold their property and possessions and willingly distributed the proceeds among themselves, ensuring everyone's needs were met. This act of sacrificial giving and communal sharing exemplified their understanding that their possessions were not their own but belonged to the community of believers.

Furthermore, the early Christians were diligent in their devotion to God. They gathered together daily in the temple, displaying a unified mindset and a shared commitment to worship and fellowship. They also gathered in homes, breaking bread together, symbolizing their shared meals and intimate connections. Their hearts were filled with gladness and sincerity as they praised God for His blessings and favor.

The impact of this genuine fellowship and selfless living was profound. The passage concludes by stating that the Lord added to the daily number of those who were being saved. The vibrant community of believers, marked by their love and generosity, became a powerful testimony to the surrounding society. Their actions attracted others to the message of salvation, resulting in more people's faith in Jesus Christ.

This passage from Acts 2:43–47 serves as an inspiring example of the early Christian community's characteristics and the impact of their unity and selfless love. It challenges us to examine our own lives and consider how we can emulate their devotion, generosity, and commitment to one another. It reminds us that when we live in harmony, care for one another, and prioritize the things of God, we become a compelling witness to the world and attract others to the saving grace of Jesus Christ.

Embracing the Oneness: Uniting in Christ's Body

When God saved three thousand souls after Peter shared a sermon on repentance and receiving the Holy Spirit, they were all given the mind of Christ, with one mind in the temple. Notice the effect it created in the early Church. They all believed in one thing, which was Christ. Then, they began to sell their property and possessions and share them among those in need.

And they were breaking the bread, eating meals, and carrying the sincerity of their hearts. What should unity look like in the Church? We have been in positions where we never took hold of honesty in our hearts. Believers are born again, and God has given them the gift of righteousness, grace, and salvation. Still, they never acknowledge the inheritance that God has given. God has gifted us, but we are never conscious of it. We tend to judge ourselves more than what He thinks of us. And I believe many Churches today highly regard the ministry more than what God has to say.

It is a dangerous position to be in. As Christians, we work to be pleased by Him, but in reality, we are already delighted by God the moment we've received Him. God has already called us sons and daughters in the kingdom. He already claims us. Whether you like it or not. The more we acknowledge what God has done and said in His Word and to us, the more we recognize who we are in Christ. And by the oracle of God, He pours His grace out so that we can walk with one mind.

In culture, it's so easy to have one mind everyone can agree on, but sometimes it isn't what Christ intended. Such as a community sharing the same mind because of culture and not walking in the fullness of God to unite the Church. To seriously lay down your life for the sake of the Gospel. In the book of Corinthians, Paul addresses that we have been joined with Christ in one flesh and one union.

The passage you mentioned is from 1 Corinthians 6:12–20. In this passage, the apostle Paul addresses the issue of sexual immorality and provides guidance to the Corinthian believers regarding their bodies and their conduct. Paul begins by acknowledging that, as believers, they have freedom in Christ.

"All things are lawful for me," he says, meaning that there are no restrictions on their freedom to engage in various activities. However, Paul emphasizes that not all things are profitable or beneficial. Although they have the freedom to do certain things, they must consider whether those actions align with God's will and contribute to their spiritual growth and well-being. Some things are pointless and not beneficial, such as playing video games. It's used for enjoyment, but it must be played in moderation. However, it's not beneficial to help grow someone in Christ.

Paul continues by highlighting the importance of not being mastered by anything. While believers are free to engage in various activities, they should not allow themselves to become controlled or enslaved by anything. They should exercise self-control and not let desire or behavior dominate their lives.

Next, Paul addresses the issue of food and the body's physical needs. He acknowledges that food is meant for the stomach, and the stomach is meant for food, emphasizing the temporary nature of material needs. However, he reminds the

Corinthians that the body is not meant for sexual immorality but is intended for the Lord. The body is a temple of the Holy Spirit; believers should honor God with their bodies.

Paul then points out the significance of the resurrection. God has raised Jesus from the dead and will also raise believers through His power. Their bodies, as members of Christ, are meant to be united with Him, and therefore, they should not engage in immoral acts that defile the body. Paul contrasts the oneness that occurs through sexual intimacy with a prostitute with the oneness believers have with the Lord. He urges them to flee from immorality and avoid sinning against their own bodies.

The passage concludes with a reminder that believers are not their own. They have been bought with a price—the precious blood of Jesus Christ—and are now temples of the Holy Spirit. Therefore, they are called to glorify God in their bodies, honoring Him with their thoughts, words, and actions.

This passage from 1 Corinthians 6:12–20 emphasizes the importance of using one's freedom in Christ wisely and responsibly. Believers are called to exercise self-control, honor God with their bodies, and flee from sexual immorality. The passage highlights the significance of the resurrection, the indwelling of the Holy Spirit, and the price paid for believers' redemption, urging them to live in a manner that brings glory to God.

You must have people involved in your life. To join in your journey as you walk with Christ. Without union, there are consequences for personal growth and being unable to see your blind spots.

Embracing Selflessness: Serving with a Kingdom Mindset

We were designed to be used by God to serve, worship, and glorify His name. I don't think it's just for us to avoid sexual immorality, and Paul would agree that it's not just avoiding sin; we are called to serve on Earth by inviting Heaven into it. Yet, there are people who continue to be selfish and look for their own paths in life. Jesus, right before His ascension, said this:

"And Jesus came up and spoke to them, saying, "All authority has been given to Me in heaven and on earth. Go therefore and make disciples of all the nations, baptizing them in the name of the Father, the Son, and the Holy Spirit, teaching them to observe all that I commanded you; and lo, I am with you always, even to the end of the age." (Matthew 28:18-20)

We are called to be disciple-makers in the kingdom. We must be aware of the people around us and take an interest in others rather than ourselves. In India, I've seen a great example of that, and I honor the people who served us. It was a blessing and a lesson to see that. And the more I witnessed how much they poured out, like Mary breaking her alabaster jar, the more their fruit was revealed through their character in Christ. And essentially, our character is essential in our lives and to His as well.

We can walk in righteousness and freedom in Christ by allowing Him to change and mold us, like a potter who shapes clay out of his hands (see Jeremiah 18 for more context). Think about this: we are called sons and daughters of the kingdom. We have received an inheritance from our Heavenly Father, who has given us the grace and power to minister to people.

Even people who need Jesus. By the blood of Jesus, we are drawn to Him. And as the body, we are called to be drawn together with complete confidence, knowing that He has the authority above every rule, dominion, power, and authority in subjection under His feet (see Ephesians 1:20-23).

We need to see a revival in the world. Think about the Day of Pentecost. Imagine that everyone would look at their hearts with humility and seek the one thing, which is Jesus. To see revival, we have to seek Him. No formulas. There are no different methods to get a revival, but we simply wait and seek His face.

It is our responsibility to look to Him when we want to help people in need, whether we're called to serve or volunteer in a Church. A judge. A teacher. A doctor.

Anything that the Lord is calling you to do and that has been brought in secret, no one would know, go for it. Your secret place is the heart of everything. No one knows. I believe that selfishness is one of the most challenging things a person can try to overcome, but we need to submit to Jesus and carry a heart of servanthood. He was a man who knew that Judas would betray him and chose to wash his feet and the disciples.

"Now before the Feast of the Passover, Jesus, knowing that His hour had come that He would depart out of this world to the Father, having loved His own who were in the world, He loved them to the end. During supper, the devil having already put into the heart of Judas Iscariot, the son of Simon, to betray Him, Jesus, knowing that the Father had given all things into His hands, and that He had come forth from God and was going

back to God, *got up from supper, and *laid aside His garments; and taking a towel, He girded Himself.

Then He *poured water into the basin, and began to wash the disciples' feet and wipe them with the towel with which He was girded. So He *came to Simon Peter. He *said to Him, "Lord, do You wash my feet?" Jesus answered and said to him, "What I do you do not realize now, but you will understand hereafter." Peter *said to Him, "Never shall You wash my feet!" Jesus answered him, "If I do not wash you, you have no part with Me." (John 13:1–7, NASB95)

Balancing Solitude and Community: Navigating the Journey of Self-Discovery and Loving Others

I remember growing up and how much of an introvert I've become. I love to spend time alone. Not to say I hate or dislike people. I wasn't much of a social person. I prefer to process and think, but it wasn't directed toward the Lord. I haven't come to know Him just yet. The issue, however, is the fact that I decided to stay alone. I'd rather spend time alone processing my thoughts and life because I want to learn more about myself. Learning and observing yourself is okay, but if it comes with isolation, then that's an issue. Isolation from people may be a form of pride.

It is interesting because we seek comfort and spend time alone instead. I feel like a hypocrite because I've done it so many times. I sometimes discern whether, in my first year of Bible school, it's okay to seek Him and sacrifice most of the hangouts my friends would do on the weekends. My heart was to seek His face, but there wasn't a conviction behind it.

Perhaps, and I had the Lord spoken through me this, but He would tell me to seek Him in secret. Before attending Bible school, my older cousin advised me to establish a secret place. This is when I was saved for only a year. A season of pursuing and seeking His love. And since then, it has been worth it; I received the rewards from the Lord, but I often ask: *"Is this wise to isolate?"* I transformed so much by seeking Him alone; I'd have a busy schedule every day, finishing school, hitting the gym, reading books, and prefer not to seek bonding time with friends, even though my most prominent love language is quality time. Yes, I saw them daily in class, saying hi, checking on them, and things like that. I believed the Lord wanted to work a lot of things in my heart. Not that I completely cut off people or don't ever hang out, but there had to be times where I needed to be present with the Lord.

I even had one or two friends ask me why I don't usually hang out with them, watching movies with the boys upstairs. I typically respond, *"Well, I want to spend time with the Lord."* Maybe they weren't interested in me, even though they were my brothers. It begs the question.

I even meditated on a book in the Bible, 1 John, about love and fellowship. I am asking the question: *"Am I loving my neighbor?" "Am I practicing the truth?"*

I don't have anything against them, but I also don't want to put a Law upon myself on why I couldn't love them the way I should intently adore them. It's not love if it's set on conditions that are required. It's pretty difficult to love, and I don't believe we can fully understand love—even considering how great His love is towards us. His love for us is what surpasses all knowledge, but we can experience that kind of love. (See Ephesians 3:19)

Regardless, we cannot promise people how to love the way they want it, even ourselves. Suppose you want to know why I focused on the Lord this school year. It wasn't because I was unloving; it was because God was teaching me about independence while being dependent on Him and on people I could trust by bringing things to light.

Before I made my second decision with Christ, I was hanging on to people when I wasn't present within myself. I was nothing. Technically, I know how to have fun with people, but it's not just love; it's being a jokester who cares less about personal growth. It was unhealthy, didn't produce fruit, and was pointless to walk in life, which didn't help me grow personally. I didn't have a job back then; I was reliant on my parents, and I walked in so much sin.

All of my friends were independent with their jobs, self-improvement, et cetera, while I was doing nothing other than being lazy and walking in sin. It wasn't a lifestyle I wanted, but I lived in fear. For years now, the Lord has radically changed my life. Physically, spiritually, mentally, and emotionally. I went from being dependent on the world to being dependent on the cross.

Rediscovering True Community: Embracing God's Perspective and the Simplicity of the Gospel

As we delve deeper into the teachings of the Bible, one thing becomes abundantly clear: our calling is to love God with all our being and to extend that love to our neighbors as ourselves. He first loved us before we loved Him (see 1 John 4:19). As I've walked alongside Him, I've witnessed tremendous growth in my own life, gradually becoming more like Him. Through this transformation, I've begun to perceive people through God's eyes—a perspective that profoundly impacts how we interact with others.

For believers, it is crucial to seek the Father in the secret place, allowing Him to instruct and guide us in the ways of love. As a unified body, we willingly lay down our lives for those around us, mirroring the sacrificial example of Christ, who gave everything for us.

"For you have been called for this purpose, since Christ also suffered for you, leaving you an example for you to follow in His steps," (1 Peter 2:21)

Embracing suffering and stepping out of our comfort zones is an integral part of our growth journey. Serving one another is an incredible honor. Loving one another is an incredible honor. And being loved by God is the greatest honor of all.

It is vital to embrace this perspective fully. If God prompts us to release someone we desire to love if the relationship isn't going well, we must let go. Not to leave in bitterness, but to choose to bless. If He directs us to love someone we may find challenging, we must extend that love. Even when faced with animosity from our enemies, we are called to respond with love. There is a supernatural power at work when we walk in the love of Christ, and it unifies and binds communities together.

Our inherent nature drives us to seek community and fulfillment. True joy cannot be found within ourselves or the world around us. Only God Himself can truly satisfy the deepest longings of our hearts. It is essential to grasp this truth and understand that genuine satisfaction can only be found in a relationship with God.

As we align ourselves with God's love and seek His guidance, we are transformed and empowered to love others selflessly. Embracing suffering and stepping out of our comfort zones is part of this journey. Serving, loving, and being loved are profound honors that bring unity and fulfillment to our lives. Ultimately, true satisfaction can only be found in a relationship with God, surpassing any worldly offering.

You can find all the drugs, all the alcohol, and yet feel unsatisfied. You can find all the books, all the studies, and all the knowledge you carry but feel unsatisfied. Why go to the length of that? A mature son would know it is not worth falling into sin, but we become captivated by curiosity. You cannot do it by yourself, but through God alone.

Community is necessary, but it should not be found outside of God. It is only found in His community. I feel that some may have been Church hurt, and it created a false view of who God is to them. It is not God nor the Church, but the sins that have dwelt among the person. A pastor may have created a false view of someone because of their sin. I believe even a person relies on the pastor more than God Himself. I noticed many people I've seen are offended by Christian terms due to their past offenses, rather than atheists or unbelievers who don't mind Christianity. We subconsciously became so fixated on the things that we believe it is okay to talk about theology rather than the simplicity of the gospel to someone.

Walking in the Power of the Spirit and Unity

For instance, evangelism or outreach is one thing that, when you go find an unbeliever, that unbeliever decides to get into a deep talk on why he believes otherwise. We fall into this trap and decide to get theological rather than walk in the power of the Spirit. The Holy Spirit is the best evangelist, and He convicts the person, not you. I'm not saying that getting into that topic is terrible; some people get saved through such conversations. But some unbelievers are blinded to the power of God. And suppose believers can acknowledge and obey the Lord in their everyday lives. How much of a transformation can a person become and those who are around? It's tempting to fall into conversations that bear no fruit, and in the end, nothing comes out other than a seed planted.

Seed planting is the best because sharing the gospel is a win-win. However, if you engage in unfruitful conversations, the unbeliever will see that Christianity is evil. It's important to know what you are called to do. The fruit comes when we abide in Jesus, and God has called us to do the work. If you pray for wisdom, you will have problems to solve. If you pray for strength, you will be tested in your spirit, man. If you pray to love, He will send your troubled hearts to love on. And so, in that, we can become more like Jesus. Don't be surprised by the trials and tribulations that come, but allow faith to build endurance in Christ.

190

Jesus' greatest prayer on unity is in the book of John. It is one of the most powerful prayers that Jesus has ever said. The entire chapter is full of gold—the unity that Jesus wanted the world to inherit from those who believed. Jesus said this for future glory:

"The glory which You have given Me I have given to them, that they may be one, just as We are one; I in them and You in Me, that they may be perfected in unity, so that the world may know that You sent Me, and loved them, even as You have loved Me. Father, I desire that they also, whom You have given Me, be with Me where I am, so that they may see My glory, which You have given Me, for You loved Me before the foundation of the world.

"O righteous Father, although the world has not known You, yet I have known You; and these have known that You sent Me; and I have made Your name known to them, and will make it known, so that the love with which You loved Me may be in them, and I in them." (John 17:22-26)

Jesus was full of glory. Perfect man. Perfect in all ways. And He desired to be with us in unity, in one flesh. This is something that we can celebrate and give thanks for. Being born again, Jesus lives inside of you. You become washed, cleansed, and purified by Him so you can be in one with Him. It is like the two became one flesh. Paul even says that the one who joins himself to the Lord is one spirit with Him (see 1 Corinthians 6:17). If this isn't something that excites you, does God Himself live inside of you? How crazy is that? Imagine everyone who walks in righteousness like Jesus. God's goal is to bring sons and daughters into the kingdom of God. That is His sovereign will for our lives. And although many things in the world continue to tempt us day by day, we have a High Priest who intercedes on our behalf to walk in the righteousness of God.

Chapter 9: The Law of Morality

Righteousness, Faith, and Walking in the Ways of God

Morality is a fundamental principle that guides righteous living, encompassing our actions and behaviors. This concept is intricately connected to the righteousness achieved through Jesus' sacrificial act on the cross. The essence of the gospel extends far beyond a mere book on moral teachings; it centers on the person of Jesus Christ, who willingly gave His life for humanity's redemption. I want to emphasize this point, even if it might sound repetitive, because it is crucial to grasp. The two foremost moral laws, as highlighted by Jesus, are to love God wholeheartedly and to love our neighbors as ourselves. These laws are not superficial quotations that we merely acknowledge; they hold profound significance and require genuine application in our lives.

Interestingly, even before God introduced His Laws to Moses and the Israelites, Abraham was credited with righteousness (as stated in Romans 4:9). This demonstrates that justice is not attained through adherence to the law alone but through faith. Abraham's righteousness was attributed to him because he believed in God and in his unwavering trust. This is a powerful reminder that our righteousness is based on faith, not on our efforts to fulfill the law. We are called to believe in Christ and live out our faith accordingly.

God has blessed Abraham to be the father of many nations, allowing us to access the Father through faith. This signifies that, through our faith in Jesus Christ, we become part of the spiritual lineage connected to Abraham. Our relationship with

God is not based on our lineage or adherence to religious rituals but on our faith in Him. By believing in Jesus Christ, we can experience the blessings and grace of God and enter into a meaningful connection with Him.

Morality goes beyond rules; it encompasses the righteousness achieved through Jesus' sacrifice. The gospel is not solely a book of moral teachings but centers on the person of Jesus Christ. The two greatest moral laws emphasize the importance of wholehearted love for God and love for others. Abraham's righteousness before the law's introduction illustrates that righteousness is attained through faith. We can access God and experience His blessings through faith, just as Abraham did.

Just after hearing from the Lord that the stars above are, how many there will be that Abraham couldn't count. We are Abraham's descendants. Abraham also did not waiver in unbelief but grew strong in faith (see Romans 4:20). It was through Abraham making the right choices that he believed that it was right to trust in what God was calling Him. It is right to see that God has called us to lay down our lives. It is simple but challenging at the same time. The Bible is the greatest source in your walk with Him. You will know that by the way you want to walk in life, which is to walk like Him.

Finding Freedom from Anxiety through Trust and Seeking God's Kingdom

Simply put, if you want to renew your mind and get set free from anxiety, many verses support that. In righteousness, God will say to you not to worry about what you will eat or what you will drink. Which is in Matthew 6 and says this:

"For this reason, I say to you, do not be worried about your life, as to what you will eat or what you will drink, nor for your body, as to what you will put on. Is not life more than food and the body more than clothing? Look at the birds of the air, that they do not sow, nor reap nor gather into barns, and yet your heavenly Father feeds them. Are you not worth much more than they? And who of you, by being worried, can add a single hour to his life? And why are you worried about clothing? Observe how the lilies of the field grow; they do not toil nor do they spin, yet I say to you that not even Solomon, in all his glory, clothed himself like one of these. But if God so clothes the grass of the field, which is alive today and tomorrow, and throws it into the furnace, will He not much more clothe you? You of little faith! Do not worry then, saying, 'What will we eat?' or 'What will we drink?' or 'What will we wear for clothing?' For the Gentiles eagerly seek all these things; for your heavenly Father knows that you need all these things. But seek first His kingdom and His righteousness, and all these things will be added to you.

"So do not worry about tomorrow; for tomorrow will care for itself. Each day has enough trouble of its own." (Matthew 6:25-34).

It holds the remedy for anxiety, echoing the very message preached by Jesus Himself. Do not allow your faith to waver! Fix your gaze upon Him, for the solution is remarkably straightforward. Yet, often, we find ourselves caught up in overanalyzing the passages bestowed upon us by God Himself. Instead, focus on seeking His kingdom and righteousness, and rest assured that everything else will naturally fall into place. Embrace the support and guidance of your fellow brothers and sisters in Christ, seeking their counsel and joining together in prayer under the influence of the Holy Spirit. In doing so, you can tap into the power of God's promised blessings, including a harmonious marriage, a thriving business, and countless other gifts. So why allow worry to consume you when the very one who holds your hand will provide the assistance and direction you need to fulfill your aspirations?

Freedom from Strongholds and Walking in Righteousness

One of the most significant battles and strongholds I faced prior to surrendering my life to Christ was the grip of pornography. It held me captive, and I struggled with this addiction. However, through the power of Christ's shed blood, I have experienced freedom from this bondage after several years. Although I stumbled during the early stages of my spiritual journey, those moments of falling into that sin became less frequent. It felt as if I had completely forgotten that such a struggle even existed. The transformative work of His blood made me new and washed me clean. Moreover, I found strength and guidance by meditating on verses that addressed the topic of temptation.

One such verse can be found in the book of Corinthians, where the apostle Paul reassures us, saying,

"No temptation has overtaken you but such as is common to man; and God is faithful, who will not allow you to be tempted beyond what you are able, but with the temptation will provide

the way of escape also, so that you will be able to endure it." (1 Corinthians 10:13).

This verse reminds us that the temptations we face are not unique to us alone; they are common to humanity. However, we can take solace in the faithfulness of God, who will never allow us to be tempted beyond our capacity to resist. In His faithfulness, He will always provide a means of escape, enabling us to endure and overcome the temptations that come our way.

This verse offers hope and encouragement to those struggling with any form of temptation, including the battle against pornography. It assures us that, with God's help, we have the strength to resist and overcome these temptations. We can find comfort in knowing that God is faithful and will always provide a way out, empowering us to endure and walk in victory.

This was the one verse that completely changed my view of how the enemy works. When you walk by the Spirit, you will know how the enemy works. Is it true that Jesus, although tempted too, has never fallen into sin. Jesus knew that the Father had provided Him a way to escape, and His grace and power equipped Him to walk in righteousness. Even Jesus has often said, *"It is written."* to the devil. It is declaring yourself by His Word that makes you walk in righteousness. It holds above every power, rule, dominion, and authority because Jesus is now seated in the heavenly places. And to back that up, here is another passage:

"I pray that the eyes of your heart may be enlightened so that you will know what is the hope of His calling, what are the

riches of the glory of His inheritance in the saints, and what is the surpassing greatness of His power toward us who believe. These are in accordance with the working of the strength of His might which He brought about in Christ when He raised Him from the dead and seated Him at His right hand in the heavenly places, far above all rule and authority and power and dominion, and every name that is named, not only in this age but also in the one to come. And He put all things in subjection under His feet and gave Him as head over all things to the Church, which is His body, the fullness of Him who fills all in all." (Ephesians 1:18-23).

Jesus has taken every power of darkness and put it in subjection under His feet. It includes your circumstances, anxieties, and the situations you have encountered that were troubling. Renewing our minds daily and acknowledging what Jesus has done and is doing as you read this book, He is Head above all things, and now is the High Priest who intercedes on our behalf so we can walk in righteousness. And the right thing to do is to believe and take action by looking into what God has called us to do. Even if life gets tough, do it with Him. By carrying the cross, you're not doing it alone. He is with you, beside you in every second of your life.

The only issue many of us struggle with is taking the *'action part.'* Do not let the things of the world hinder your calling, which God is calling you to do. It may be in business, ministry, or looking out for troubled hearts. Our general right to live is to follow Him. Francis Schaeffer said this quote that hits this chapter:

"The moral absolutes rest upon God's character. The moral commands He has given to men are an expression of His character. Men, as created in His image, are to live by choice on the basis of what God is. The standards of morality are determined by what conforms to His character, while those things which do not conform are immoral." – Francis Schaeffer.

We were created in His image and have been given a choice. Romans 12:2 says not to conform to this world, but that the renewal of our minds transforms us. We must persevere to end up in His image: His likeness, character, and many more. It points us toward the finished work on the cross. In that way, we can live in a place of rest.

Submission to Authority: Embracing God's Design for Order and Peace

Throughout our lives, it is inevitable that we will stumble and make mistakes. While we cannot guarantee perfection, we can recognize that following Jesus wholeheartedly is the best decision we can make. In my journey, I used to harbor a fear of self-condemnation, believing every mistake I made would lead to eternal judgment. These lies plagued me daily, preventing me from finding peace within myself. However, after recommitting my life to Christ, I discovered that God is an extraordinary counselor, offering guidance and comfort like no other. It is crucial to reach out to our fellow brothers and sisters in Christ because they, too, possess the mind of Christ, just as we do. However, one of the challenges we may encounter is struggling to trust those around us.

In Romans 13, the apostle Paul addresses the governing authorities in Rome, explaining the importance of submitting to their authority. He emphasizes that all authority ultimately comes from God, as He is the one who establishes it. This passage is significant, particularly as it relates to the law of morality. Paul states that every person should be subject to the governing authorities, and resisting authority is essentially opposing God's ordained order. Those who oppose authority will face condemnation. Rulers are meant to instill fear in those who engage in evil behavior, not in those who do good. If we desire to have no fear of authority, we should strive to do what is right and commendable, as rulers serve as ministers of God for our well-being. However, if we engage in evil, we should be afraid, as God appoints rulers to punish those who practice wrongdoing. It is, therefore, necessary to submit not just out of fear of punishment but also for the sake of our conscience.

Paul further explains that paying taxes is an obligation because rulers are servants of God, devoting themselves to their responsibilities. We must fulfill our obligations by rendering what is due, including taxes, customs, fear, and honor. The only thing we should owe others is love for one another. When we love our neighbors, we fulfill the law, which includes commandments such as not committing adultery, not murdering, not stealing, and not coveting. All commandments are summed up in the saying, *"Love your neighbor as yourself."* Love does not harm a neighbor, so when we truly love, we fully embody the essence of the law.

This passage from Romans 13 reminds us of the importance of submitting to governing authorities and recognizing their role as established by God. It also emphasizes the significance of love in fulfilling the law, as genuine love for one another encompasses all the commandments. By understanding and applying these principles, we can navigate our relationship with authority, fulfill our obligations, and live out the love that Christ has called us to demonstrate.

"Every person is to be in subjection to the governing authorities. For there is no authority except from God, and those which exist are established by God. Therefore, whoever resists authority has opposed the ordinance of God, and they who have opposed will receive condemnation upon themselves. For rulers are not a cause of fear for good behavior but for evil. Do you want to have no fear of authority? Do what is good, and you will have praise from the same, for it is a minister of God to you for good. But if you do what is evil, be afraid; for it does not bear the sword for nothing; for it is a minister of God, an avenger who brings wrath on the one who practices evil. Therefore, it is necessary to be in subjection, not only because of wrath but also for conscience's sake. For because of this, you also pay taxes, for rulers are servants of God, devoting themselves to this very thing. Render to all what is due them: tax to whom tax is due; custom to whom custom; fear to whom fear; honor to whom honor.

Owe nothing to anyone except to love one another, for he who loves his neighbor has fulfilled the law. For this, "You shall not commit adultery, You shall not murder, You shall not steal, You shall not covet," and if there is any other commandment, it is summed up in this saying, "You shall love your neighbor as yourself." Love does no wrong to a neighbor; therefore, love is the fulfillment of the law. (Romans 13:1-9).

Authority is always a part of our lives. Someone is always above you, or someone is below you. It includes family members, the president, children, et cetera. God has the highest authority in our lives. In the beginning, God created the heavens and the earth. Paul says that if we resist the authority the people have placed on us, we also oppose God's ordinance. Now it's not to say that we submit to people who abuse power and bring destruction, just like the many kings in the Old Testament who have done that. We have the authority that God has given us to flee from temptation, whether we're unbelievers or believers. Even an unbeliever can run from temptation through secular methods, but there's no presence, no secure salvation. Authority has been in our nature since we were born. The purpose of this passage is that God has designed authority to ensure evil doesn't spread. The Bible says there is no condemnation in Christ Jesus. Still, we have to be aware of the earthly consequences that are against the ordinance of God, especially what is sinful. Human government is needed because it restrains the influence of evil in this world.

Therefore, we do not fear the higher people; instead, we can trust those walking in righteousness and those running our world (such as the president). Christians are called to do good according to what He says. God is a *just* God. There is no unrighteousness or unfairness in His eyes. We must submit ourselves to Christ by submitting to the things held higher than us. We don't rebel, but the Spirit leads us.

It is the right thing to do because, if not, we will live in fear of where we are. Christians during that time were taxpayers because those taxes supported the work God intended to do through human authorities. We must work together and build communities based on what God intends. To prevent evil and bring peace in His name. Honor who you honor. Fear to whom fear (respect) regards who is above or below you in authority. God's design is to bring peace and reverence to those around us.

The Law of Human Nature: Understanding Our Tendency to Fall and Struggle with Moral Choices

Guard yourself against the lure of temptation and avoid misusing your authority. Refuse to allow the enemy to gain control over you, for in reality, he has no power over you. Likewise, do not abuse the authority entrusted to you by God over others. Remember that only Christ possesses perfect authority; through Him, we can find access and confidence. Release your grip on things you hold dear but that God calls you to let go of.

Do not procrastinate in fulfilling the tasks and responsibilities God has assigned you. Even if it seems mundane, discipline yourself and commit to prayer, studying God's Word, taking charge of your life, and addressing your issues. The law of morality requires us to wholeheartedly follow God and offer ourselves entirely to Him. Dedicating our flesh to the altar daily, represented by the cross, is key. Dying to myself. Act promptly to fulfill God's calling on your life, as doing so will bring you closer to fulfilling His divine destiny. Neglecting to follow God's

Word will only lead to further deception by the enemy, causing you to stumble more. Remember that your true identity belongs to Christ, and obeying the One who created you is crucial.

However, we often struggle to align our actions with what we know is right, and our mistakes can hinder us. The law of human nature pertains to the behavior we naturally expect from ourselves and others. This knowledge is ingrained in us due to our personal history and background. We may assume that people should understand certain things based on their experiences. It involves the concepts of right and wrong, good and evil. As C.S. Lewis discusses in *'Mere Christianity,'* the law of human nature encompasses our built-in expectations to fulfill our needs. Yet, it often leads to disappointment when these expectations clash with the flawed aspects of human nature. We inherently understand this law, and it governs our moral compass. It is a self-explanatory law inherent in our human nature.

Even dropping a stone from our hands will guarantee it will fall because the stone, by nature, knows the law of gravity and the law of nature. But why is it that we make mistakes and say to ourselves, *"We knew about this, and yet we make the same mistake we told ourselves we wouldn't make,"* or *"That guy didn't fulfill my needs; I thought he was going to do it, but now I'm disappointed."* That is, we *create* the measure of our standard based on the circumstances of the law, which is called the law of decent behavior and moral law. *"You knew better"* or *"I should have known better."* It is what we do and live, yet we make the mistake of not doing it. It is that we *create* laws for ourselves. The same applies in Christian theology, that sin reigns on Earth like the Law of Gravity, that we break the law of human nature without knowing we did.

Grace Over Law: Embracing the New Covenant and Living in the Power of Christ

As prophesied by Jeremiah and mentioned earlier in the book, the laws are now written in our minds and hearts, allowing Christ to dwell within us (Hebrews 8:7–13). It is the new covenant, rendering the old one obsolete. The Man who entered this world came to triumph over the Law by embodying the Law Himself and fulfilling all its requirements. He, who was without sin, took on our sin on our behalf (2 Corinthians 5:21), and in doing so, He transcended the confines of the Law. Through Him, we have complete access to the divine nature of God. It is why we no longer live under the Law but in the empowering grace of God. It is finished because, by grace, we have been saved through faith in the finished work of the cross. We receive grace as a gift, enabling us to become like Him and act accordingly. It is a matter of belief and living out that belief in our daily lives.

Jesus isn't an accuser but instead a Judge, a righteous one. He didn't come to be one, but rather to save. Look at the story with the adulterer. Jesus was on the Mount of Olives, and the scribes and Pharisees brought in a woman caught in adultery. They all point at this woman at her in that she should be condemned. At this moment, it was a test to Jesus to see if they could find any accusation. The Law of Moses said that a woman such as this would be stoned to have grounds to accuse Him.

It is how the spirit of accusation works: by charging the one who was caught, also blame the one who claimed to be God. We accuse, and then it spreads to those around us like a virus. Imagine all the things you have done to spread such misinformation. They get passed from one to another. Jesus, at the moment, had every person who was pointing at the woman to themselves because they were accused of their sins and said, "He who is without sin among you, let him be the first to throw a stone at her."

Next thing you know, the oldest and the youngest started to withdraw individually. All that was left were Jesus and the adulterous woman. Jesus had every right to throw the stone at her, but the law of morality and the right thing to do is simply to say, *"Go and sin no more."* No longer do you have to go through condemnation. No more do you have to sin. Why? Because He, above all things, believes that we deserve life in Him. He's the giver of life.

"You are the giver of life. Your light lets us enjoy life." (Psalms 36:9 NCV)

He has not only taken every sin upon Himself and left it in the grave, but He has resurrected. And with the mind of Christ, we can experience what He has gone through in the Spirit. Here are the seven confessions of the faith, and these are such:

1. I have been called by God (Romans 1:7).

2. I have been crucified with Christ (Galatians 2:20).

3. I have been buried with Christ (Colossians 3:3).

4. I have been resurrected with Christ (Romans 6:5).

5. I have been raised with Christ (Colossians 3:1).

6. I have been seated with Christ (Ephesians 2:6).

7. I will be ready for Christ's return (Luke 12:35–37).

Surrendering All: Embracing Humility and Finding Strength in Christ's Love

It is an honor to know that He lives in us so that we become perfect in Him every day. And it is up to you how far you want to go. How much of a measure will you give so He can pour His Spirit upon you? It is worth going for it. If you need to break, break yourself. If you need to mourn, mourn. If you need to grieve, grieve. But in all things you do, good or bad, do it with Him. He is there with you in every step of your life.

In my personal journey, I vividly recall reaching a point where external appearances and the opinions of others held no sway over me. I cared not for the unrighteous judgments or negative words that might be spoken. The way I presented myself to others became inconsequential. I resolved not to allow the fear of man or anything that did not align with God's will to have a hold on my life. As long as I had Him, that was all that truly mattered.

I can still recall a profound question posed to me by my youngest cousin, one that invites introspection and reveals the depth of our faith. They asked, "If you were to lose everything in your life—your home, your friends, your family, essentially everything—would you still find satisfaction in Him?" While many would readily respond with a resounding "yes," it is crucial to examine the actual state of our hearts. It is easy to utter those words, but what truly rests within your heart at this very moment? Is Christ genuinely the Lord and King of your life?

In moments like these, let us turn to the book of Job and consider the trials and tribulations he endured. Despite his immense challenges, he allowed God to reign supreme in his life. Even if it appeared foolish to others, he surrendered to the lordship of God. Therefore, let us find joy amid the trials and tribulations that may come our way. Let us anchor ourselves in His Word, continually renew our minds, and conform to His will. This way, even if we were to lose everything, we could still experience deep and abiding joy.

Consider Peter in this passage:

"You younger men, likewise, be subject to your elders; and all of you, clothe yourselves with humility toward one another, for God is opposed to the proud, but gives grace to the humble. Therefore, humble yourselves under the mighty hand of God, that He may exalt you at the proper time, casting all your anxiety on Him because He cares for you. Be of sober spirit; be on the alert. Your adversary, the devil, prowls around like a roaring lion, seeking someone to devour. But resist him, firm in your faith, knowing that the same experiences of suffering are being accomplished by your brethren who are in the world. After you have suffered for a little while, the God of all grace, who called you to His eternal glory in Christ, will Himself perfect, confirm, strengthen, and establish you. To Him be dominion forever and ever. Amen." (1 Peter 5:5–11)

Honor to whom honor, fear to whom fear, render what is due, custom to whom custom. And to add on, submit to whomever submits. Which is Christ Jesus. Do what it takes to walk in righteousness by giving everything you can to Him. He will provide you with strength and power because He loves you.

Chapter 10: Beholding the One

Beholding the Works of Christ: Unveiling the Ninefold Manifestations of His Power

Behold! Let us fix our gaze on the One who descended from above. A profound quote by William Blake, *"We become what we behold,"* has resonated with me countless times, for its truthfulness is undeniable. In the tapestry of our lives, there is something we behold each and every day. The Greek word *"ide,"* meaning *"behold,"* calls us to truly see and take notice. Behold! Look! As we fix our gaze upon Jesus, our hearts align with the profound truth within us. We are summoned to behold the entirety of Christ's work, not merely a single facet such as the crucifixion, although that is undeniably significant. Jesus is preparing a table for us when He comes back. The Marriage of the Lamb:

"Let us rejoice and be glad and give the glory to Him, for the marriage of the Lamb has come and His bride has made herself ready." It was given to her to clothe herself in fine linen, bright and clean, for the fine linen is the righteous acts of the saints. Then he *said to me, "Write, 'Blessed are those who are invited to the marriage supper of the Lamb.'" And he *said to me, "These are the true words of God." Then I fell at his feet to worship him. But he *said to me, "Do not do that; I am a fellow servant of yours and your brethren who hold the testimony of Jesus; worship God. For the testimony of Jesus is the spirit of prophecy." (Revelation 12:7-10)

There are the *"ninefold works of Christ."* The first work is the incarnation of Jesus becoming human and taking on flesh to live among us through the Holy Spirit through Mary, the mother of Jesus. The next one was the Messianic Mission, with Jesus fulfilling the Old Testament prophecies and serving as the promised Messiah.

The Transformative Power of Beholding the Finished Work of the Cross

The one I want to focus on next is the work of the cross, His third work. When Jesus said His last words, He said, *"It is finished."* We look at what He has done in our lives by acknowledging that He has taken every sin, sickness, and even death. He was beaten, whipped, mocked, and pulled from his beard in every way possible. He was unrecognizable to others. Isaiah 52:14 (NIV) says,

"Just as there were many who were appalled at him, his appearance was so disfigured beyond that of any human being and his form was marred beyond human likeness."

Jesus fulfilled the prophecy spoken by Isaiah, a testament to the brutal mistreatment He endured during His time on Earth. Isaiah 53, an entire chapter dedicated to Jesus, depicts Him as the sacrificial lamb led to slaughter. Despite the unjust accusations and afflictions, Jesus remained silent, bearing the weight of our transgressions and removing every judgment against us. This profound truth is drawn from Isaiah 53.

Now, why is this of utmost significance to us? Jesus endured the most agonizing death imaginable. He was mercilessly scourged, beaten, and ultimately crucified, enduring six excruciating hours on the cross. In contrast to the animals sacrificed under the old covenant, which provided temporary atonement for sin, Jesus offered Himself as the ultimate and complete sacrifice for our sins. We no longer need to strive to overcome our sins when we can simply behold the finished work of the cross. It was the most monumental sacrifice humanity has ever witnessed. Now, all we need to do is fix our gaze upon our King, who triumphantly rose from the grave three days later, conquering death itself. We need not rely on external circumstances or attempt to rid ourselves of sin through our own efforts and spiritual activities.

We are transformed and radiant by beholding Him with His love and compassion. I earnestly wish it were easier to convey His character's goodness. However, our struggle lies in the unbelief that stems from this fallen world. We often compare our experiences and allow the lies we encounter to diminish the sufficiency of God's love due to our own sins. We tend to view ourselves as flawed, unworthy, and imperfect. And indeed, we are broken. Yet, we have been redeemed and cleansed by the precious Blood of Jesus. His Blood is the most powerful and the only means by which we gain access to the Father. He is pleased with us, regardless of our thoughts or self-perception. And by simply beholding His finished work, we begin to grasp the depth of His love for us. We are forgiven of our sins and reconciled to God through faith in Jesus and His sacrifice on the cross. Romans 5:10 says:

"For if while we were enemies we were reconciled to God through the death of His Son, much more, having been reconciled, we shall be saved by His life." (Romans 5:10)

Embracing the Symbolism of Burial: A Proclamation of New Life

Now, if you look carefully at His finished works, the cross is not the only thing to behold. We can also behold the burial. The burial is where a righteous man named Joseph, a council member from Arimathea, laid Jesus in the tomb. Joseph took the body of Jesus after receiving approval from Pilate to bury it in the grave by wrapping Jesus up in linen cloth. (see Luke 23:50–54).

What we can behold from this burial is looking at what Paul had to say:

"What shall we say then? Are we to continue in sin so that grace may increase? May it never be! How shall we who died to sin still live in it? Or do you not know that all of us who have been baptized into Christ Jesus have been baptized into His death? Therefore, we have been buried with Him through baptism into death, so that as Christ was raised from the dead through the glory of the Father, so we too might walk in the newness of life." (Romans 6:1-4).

Upon experiencing the transformative rebirth in Christ, as a believer, it is crucial to undergo the sacrament of water baptism. This act serves as a declaration to those who witness it and to the Lord Himself, signifying your wholehearted commitment to follow Jesus and be cleansed of your sins. Referencing Acts 2:38 and Acts 22:16, we find the scriptural basis for being baptized for the remission of our sins.

"Corresponding to that, baptism now saves you—not the removal of dirt from the flesh, but an appeal to God for a good

conscience—through the resurrection of Jesus Christ, who is at the right hand of God, having gone into heaven, after angels and authorities and powers had been subjected to Him." (1 Peter 3:21–22)

In the profound moment of being born again, water baptism allows you to identify with the mind of Christ. As you descend into the water, symbolically mirroring the laying of Jesus in the tomb, you are immersed in His burial. When you rise out of the water, it parallels His victorious resurrection from the dead. This symbolic act holds immense spiritual significance and grants you a profound rest in Christ, forever transforming your life. Through water baptism, we can behold the burial of Jesus, recognizing how He buried our sins in the grave and vanquished the enemy in the depths of hell.

Moreover, Jesus' burial serves as the fulfillment of a prophecy found in Isaiah 53, which speaks of Him being laid to rest in a tomb belonging to a wealthy man, namely Joseph:

"His grave was assigned with wicked men, yet He was with a rich man in His death because He had done no violence, nor was there any deceit in His mouth" (Isaiah 53:9).

This prophetic fulfillment further underscores the profound significance of Jesus' burial, highlighting His innocence and the honor bestowed upon Him even in His death.

Thus, water baptism stands as a powerful testimony of our faith, aligning us with the death, burial, and resurrection of our Lord Jesus Christ and granting us a deep understanding of the redemptive work accomplished on our behalf.

Embracing the Power of Resurrection: A New Life in Christ

The next one is the resurrection, as I mentioned about being raised from the water in baptism. We leave our sins and old lifestyles behind and are raised with Christ. This correlates with the crucifixion. I have been crucified with Christ; it is not I who live, but Christ that lives in me (see Galatians 2:20). When we look at the resurrection, every single thing the enemy has done in our lives has been left in the grave. Now, you have been brought alive with Jesus in His resurrection. It is straightforward. You're dead to sin and alive to God. Paul said this in Romans:

"But if the Spirit of Him who raised Jesus from the dead dwells in you, He who raised Christ Jesus from the dead will also give life to your mortal bodies through His Spirit who dwells in you." (Romans 8:11)

Our mortal bodies in this world affect us in our walk in life. Everywhere you see around you is corrupted by everything, whether it's from your relationships or the influence of drugs and alcohol, even pornography and self-indulging and prosperous things around the world. As I said, I don't believe secular things such as music or movies are bad. God may speak to you through that, but if the Holy Spirit convicts you, you must withdraw from those things and obey Him. Jesus, when He rose from the dead, He now dwells in you by receiving Him in your life. You have been raised with Him, and His Spirit now resides in you. And with the Spirit of God, you can walk in His righteousness. We cannot rely on and look within ourselves to solve the issues. You may find all the peace, humility, and patience, but you cannot find them anywhere other than Christ

Himself. And the resurrection is what we hold fast to. Another passage to look at is knowing to set your minds on things that are above and not on Earth; you have been raised with Christ, and you desire things that are of Him:

Therefore, if you have been raised up with Christ, keep seeking the things above, where Christ is, seated at the right hand of God. Set your mind on the things above, not the things on earth. For you have died, and your life is hidden with Christ in God. When Christ, who is our life, is revealed, then you also will be revealed with Him in glory. (Colossians 3:1-4)

In the book of Corinthians, Paul preached to the Corinth Church that people must hold fast to the Truth when they have received the gospel.

"Now I make known to you, brethren, the gospel which I preached to you, which also you received, in which also you stand, by which also you are saved if you hold fast the word which I preached to you unless you believed in vain. For I delivered to you as of first importance what I also received, that Christ died for our sins according to the Scriptures and that He was buried, and that He was raised on the third day according to the Scriptures" (1 Corinthians 15:1-4).

And in the same chapter:

"Now, if Christ is preached, that He has been raised from the dead, how do some among you say that there is no resurrection of the dead? But if there is no resurrection of the dead, not even Christ has been raised; and if Christ has not been raised, then our preaching is vain, your faith also is vain. Moreover, we are even found to be false witnesses of God because we testified

against God that He raised Christ, whom He did not raise, if, in fact, the dead are not raised. For if the dead are not raised, not even Christ has been raised; and if Christ has not been raised, your faith is worthless; you are still in your sins. Then those also who have fallen asleep in Christ have perished. If we have hoped in Christ in this life only, we are of all men most to be pitied." (1 Corinthians 15:12–19)

Suppose you look as you read the entire chapter of 1 Corinthians 15. In that case, you will start seeing Christ's resurrection's importance. You will begin to behold and celebrate what the Lord has done. You will start to become alive with Him and be dead to your sin.

You will start to transform when you begin to behold His resurrection. Instead of looking at yourself, your issues, and your struggles, you will behold Him, and His grace and power will come into you. You will feel more at peace than anything you have ever received. However, if you notice that you have fallen into sin or perhaps don't feel at ease, simply behold Him. Paul said in the book of Ephesians that we, as the body, may be enlightened.

"I pray that the eyes of your heart may be enlightened so that you will know what the hope of His calling is, what are the riches of the glory of His inheritance in the saints, and what is the surpassing greatness of His power toward us who believe. These are in accordance with the working of the strength of His might which He brought about in Christ when He raised Him from the dead and seated Him at His right hand in the heavenly places, far above all rule and authority and power and dominion, and every name that is named, not only in this age

but also in the one to come. And He put all things in subjection under His feet, and gave Him as head over all things to the Church, which is His body, the fullness of Him who fills all in all." (Ephesians 1:18-23)

In the same way, Moses lifted the serpent in the wilderness so that the Son of Man would be lifted (see John 3:14). In the book of Numbers, after the Lord sent fiery serpents and bit people, they would die. The people of Israel were led out of the wilderness and walked in disobedience to God and Moses.

People complained that they were brought from Egypt and believed they would die in the wilderness without food. There was a time when the people of Israel sinned and spoke against the Lord. The people of Israel asked Moses to intercede on their behalf, so Moses made a bronze serpent and set it up so that they would live when people looked at the serpent. (see Numbers 21:4–9)

Do you see that people have complained at this time? Understandably, no food or water was provided, but they sinned against the Lord. You can be angry and not sin (see Ephesians 4:26–27). And in this example, God has set them free from the four hundred and thirty years of slavery in Egypt and made them ungrateful for what He has done for them. You may be in the same position, you feel unappreciated, and God has not blessed you in areas you wish He would have done. But it's not about your circumstances or how you view the situation. God is above all things; He has one of the best plans no man would make for themselves. And when you submit and behold His finished work, you will see God move more than you have probably ever seen. And Jesus humbled Himself by becoming obedient to the point of death.

"Being found in appearance as a man, He humbled Himself by becoming obedient to the point of death, even death on a cross. For this reason, also, God highly exalted Him and bestowed on Him the name which is above every name, so that at the name of Jesus every knee will bow, of those who are in heaven and on earth and under the earth, and that every tongue will confess that Jesus Christ is Lord, to the glory of God the Father." (Philippians 2:8-11)

Ascending to Glory: The Triumph of Jesus and His Eternal Reign

Following His resurrection, Jesus spent forty days with His disciples, providing undeniable proof of His victory over death by revealing His pierced hands, feet, and sides, even showing Himself to Thomas. Jesus made a profound statement in John 3:13, declaring that no one has ascended into heaven except the Son of Man, who descended from heaven. In the Gospel of Luke, Jesus appeared in their midst as the disciples gathered, offering them His peace. Although we may feel apprehensive since we cannot physically see Him with our eyes, it is through faith that we receive His peace. We can confidently acknowledge and access this peace, knowing it is available.

Moreover, Jesus promised to send the Helper, the Holy Spirit, as stated in John 16. When the Holy Spirit dwells within us, we can continually behold Jesus. This is not limited to mere prayers or seeking Him out of boredom; instead, the Holy Spirit draws us near to Him and ignites a hunger to know Him more.

Through the Holy Spirit, we receive divine power and grow in Christlikeness. The disciples feared that once Jesus ascended to heaven, they would lose access to Him. However, with the indwelling of the Holy Spirit, our connection with Him remains unbroken, and we have constant access to His presence.

By relying on the Holy Spirit, we can behold Jesus without ceasing, experiencing His love, guidance, and transformation in our lives. The gift of the Holy Spirit ensures that we are never separated from the presence of our Savior, and we can intimately commune with Him at all times.

In the following few chapters of John 20, Jesus breathed the Holy Spirit into the disciples right before He went up. This ascension was significant because Jesus fulfilled a prophecy that foretold His ascension. In Psalms 68:18, it says this:

"When you ascended to the heights, you led a crowd of captives. You received gifts from the people, even from those who rebelled against you. Now the Lord God will live among us there." (Psalms 68:18 NLT)

Even in Daniel, he saw a vision of the Son of Man receiving dominion and that He received power and glory:

"I kept looking in the night visions, And behold, with the clouds of heaven One like a Son of Man was coming, And He came up to the Ancient of Days And was presented before Him. And to Him was given dominion, Glory and a kingdom, That all the peoples, nations and men of every language Might serve Him. His dominion is an everlasting dominion Which will not pass away, And His kingdom is one Which will not be destroyed." (Daniel 7:13-14)

This passage from Daniel was one of the most prophetic words he has received, saying that Jesus was to be exalted and given authority by the Father. Matthew says that even the Son of Man would come in the clouds of heaven with power and great glory (see Matthew 24:30). When you know that the Father has given Jesus everything, you behold His ascension and begin to thank Him. In the first chapter of the book of Acts, Jesus ascended, and two men in white clothing stood beside the disciples, saying that Jesus had been taken up into heaven. (see Acts 1:9–11).

The Enthronement of Jesus: Majesty, Power, and the Hope of His Return

The following subsequent work was Jesus' enthronement in heaven. We can behold His enthronement because of His majesty and power on His throne. Jesus is seated at the Father's right hand, and He has given him all authority in heaven and on earth (see Matthew 28:18). Jesus has been with God since before creation existed. He is the King of our lives. He is the Lord of our lives. Jesus had a perfect life for thirty-three years, and He died on the cross for our sins; therefore, He is now seated in the heavenly places. Paul said that we believers are co-heirs with Christ (see Romans 8:17) and that when He comes back, He will share His glory when He returns on a white horse. (See Colossians 3:4). Therefore, we behold Jesus after He took over every principality, rule, dominion, and power and put things under subjection so we could live in power with Him. We have guaranteed hope and a future that we are secure in Him.

As you behold Him, the Holy Spirit will give you the grace and power to be excited about His return!

The High Priestly Role of Jesus: Mediator, Intercessor, and the Power of His Blood

The next and current work we are in is Jesus being the High Priest. Jesus has become our mediator and intercessor before God. Every single second of your life, you are being prayed over by Jesus to be drawn near Him (see Hebrews 8:34). His blood covers the mercy seat. The Father looks over that His blood was spilled so that everyone is forgiven of sins. The blood never gets cold or dry. This doesn't mean you're saved; you must repent, see the truth, and accept Jesus. God says to the world that people are forgiven but must repent and see Him rightly. The main point is that we have a High Priest who has taken His seat at the right hand of God (see Hebrews 8:1 and Romans 8:34).

Therefore, since we have a great high priest who has passed through the heavens, Jesus the Son of God, let us hold fast our confession. For we do not have a high priest who cannot sympathize with our weaknesses, but One who has been tempted in all things as we are, yet without sin. Therefore, let us draw near with confidence to the throne of grace so that we may receive mercy and find grace to help in time of need. (Hebrews 4:14-16)

Even John said that we have an advocate with the Father, Jesus Christ, who is righteous. He gives His power to not stumble and fall into sin (see 1 John 2:1). The nature of the High Priest is that Jesus came down in the flesh to come and destroy the power of darkness. He was tempted for you, yet without sin, so that you wouldn't sin anymore. He is merciful and faithful and became a propitiation of our sins to help those tempted. (see Hebrews 2:17–18).

There is a simple yet powerful truth during moments of doubt and trouble: we can behold Jesus as our High Priest, interceding on our behalf. In doing so, we find solace and rest in His faithful promises, which are revealed through the Word. It is essential to recognize that Jesus did not appoint Himself as the High Priest; rather, it was God who bestowed this honor upon Him.

In the Old Testament, the role of the High Priest held tremendous significance. Once a year, on the Day of Atonement, the High Priest would enter the holy of holies in the Tabernacle of Moses, offering sacrifices for the sins of the entire camp of Israel. If you were to ask a High Priest of that time, they would provide detailed instructions on the sacred duties they had to fulfill in service to God.

The Holy of Holies housed the Ark of the Covenant, which contained the mercy seat. It was a sacred space where anyone entering with any impurity in their spirit, soul, or body would face death in the presence of God. It was because God is pure, perfect in every way, and radiates pure light.

Here lies the extraordinary truth: we have a High Priest who not only speaks on behalf of humanity but also grants us direct access to God. Understanding the significance of Jesus' role as our intercessor should instill profound confidence and rest within us. He intercedes for us daily, bridging the gap between us and God and ensuring we can approach the Almighty with assurance and trust.

If we truly grasp the importance of Jesus' intercession on our behalf, we will find an abundance of confidence and rest in Him. Through His role as High Priest, we can approach God, knowing that our prayers and needs are presented before His throne. This truth should fill our hearts with gratitude and bring us into a deeper sense of peace and assurance in our relationship with Him. Hebrews says that people have become dull at hearing:

"Concerning him, we have much to say concerning him, and it is hard to explain since you have become dull of hearing. For though by this time you ought to be teachers, you have need again for someone to teach you the elementary principles of the oracles of God, and you have come to need milk and not solid food. For everyone who partakes only of milk is not accustomed to the word of righteousness, for he is an infant. But solid food is for the mature, who, because of practice, have their senses trained to discern good and evil." (Hebrews 5:11-14).

The dullness of hearing keeps us from going deeper into the gospel and capturing the complete revelation of truth that is revealed to us. Suppose you could believe what Jesus is doing on your behalf. Not your theological ways, but what is the biblical foundation on which He is praying for you right now? Is He praying that your faith won't waver? Is He praying that your family members will be saved? There are many things for which He is praying that you will be drawn near to Him daily. He has sprinkled His blood on the mercy seat so that the Father will forgive you of your sins. Jesus has not only done this, but He has also given us rest.

Therefore, let us fear if, while a promise remains of entering His rest, any one of you may seem to have come short of it. For indeed we have had good news preached to us, just as they also; but the word they heard did not profit them, because it was not united by faith in those who heard. For we who have believed enter that rest, just as He has said, "As I swore in My wrath, They shall not enter My rest," although His works were finished from the foundation of the world. For He has said somewhere concerning the seventh day: "And God rested on the seventh day from all His works,"; and again in this passage, "They shall not enter My rest." Therefore, since it remains for some to enter it, and those who formerly had good news preached to them failed to enter because of disobedience, He again fixes a certain day, "Today," saying through David after so long a time just as has been said before, "Today if you hear His voice, Do not harden your hearts." (Hebrews 4:1-7)

There is rest when you know He has given you promises that what you have been praying for is in His will. He may say yes, no, or not yet, but His plans are perfect. Not only can you trust His plans for your life, but you can also rest by simply being still and knowing He's God. We don't have to work or strive to receive Him because we already have Him for those who receive Him. And now that we can be diligent to enter that rest, no one will fall into sin, following the same example of disobedience (see Hebrews 4:11). The author of Hebrews said that we take care of ourselves so well that no one would walk in unbelief.

"Take care, brethren, that there not be in any one of you an evil, unbelieving heart that falls away from the living God. But

encourage one another day after day, as long as it is still called "Today," so that none of you will be hardened by the deceitfulness of sin. For we have become partakers of Christ if we hold fast the beginning of our assurance firm until the end," (Hebrews 3:12-14)

Preparing for the Glorious Return: The Bridegroom and the Final Work

The last and final work to come is The Bridegroom. It produces a life of purity. Behold the wedding that He is returning to get His bride and be united. Purity is so vital to walking with God. It's purity that meets the same standard as Christ. The glorious return of Jesus is mentioned in the Book of Matthew:

"But immediately after the tribulation of those days, the sun will be darkened, and the moon will not give its light, and the stars will fall from the sky, and the powers of the heavens will be shaken. And then the sign of the Son of Man will appear in the sky, and then all the tribes of the earth will mourn, and they will see the Son of Man coming on the clouds of the sky with power and great glory. And He will send forth His angels with a great trumpet, and they will gather together His elect from the four winds, from one end of the sky to the other." (Matthew 24:29-31)

The reference you will notice is prophesied from Isaiah 13, as many, such as Joel 2:31 and Amos 8:9, describe the day of the Lord as a future event that will bring judgment upon the Earth, but most importantly, the Son of Man comes back to unite with

His bride. Several scriptures involve the Son of Man coming on a cloud, such as Daniel (7:13–14).

"I kept looking in the night visions, And behold, with the clouds of heaven One like a Son of Man was coming, And He came up to the Ancient of Days And was presented before Him. "And to Him was given dominion, Glory and a kingdom, That all the peoples, nations and men of every language Might serve Him. His dominion is an everlasting dominion Which will not pass away; And His kingdom is one, Which will not be destroyed."

Jesus has been given authority by God the Father to destroy sin forever when He returns and establishes His eternal kingdom. As for us, sometimes we may feel troubled by the challenges we face in our daily lives. It can be easy to forget the faith that Jesus has in us and the power He gives us to overcome these challenges. Just like the work of the High Priest, we need to remember and have faith in the power of Jesus to guide us. He promised our hearts would not be troubled if we simply believed in Him. We must remember the promises that He has given us to rest upon. We cannot ignore the finished work of the cross that brings rest, and Jesus said this to encourage our hearts:

*"Do not let your heart be troubled; believe in God, believe also in Me. In My Father's house are many dwelling places; if it were not so, I would have told you, for I go to prepare a place for you. If I go and prepare a place for you, I will come again and receive you to Myself, that where I am, there you may be also. And you know the way where I am going." Thomas *said to Him, "Lord, we do not know where You are going; how do we know*

the way?" Jesus *said to him, "I am the way, and the truth, and the life; no one comes to the Father but through Me." (John 14:1-6).

The Betrothal: A Willing Commitment and Spiritual Cleansing

He has a place for us—where we can be united with Him. There were three orders in traditional Jewish weddings back in the days of Jesus. The first is the "Shiddunkhin." [1] *"Then the Lord God said, "It is not good for the man to be alone; I will make him a helper suitable for him." (Genesis 2:18)*

In Jewish culture, matchmaking is called "*Shiddukhin*," which can be compared to modern-day dating and mutual commitment. According to tradition, the father must find a suitable partner for his son by carefully considering their needs and preferences. Once the right match is identified, the couple is introduced and allowed to get to know each other. They may become engaged and eventually get married if they both feel compatible. This practice is also mentioned in the Bible, where Abraham helped his son Isaac find a spouse by sending out his servant to find a suitable match.

Now Abraham was old, advanced in age, and the Lord had blessed Abraham in every way. Abraham said to his servant, the oldest of his household, who had charge of all that he owned, "Please place your hand under my thigh, and I will make you swear by the Lord, the God of heaven and the God of earth, that you shall not take a wife for my son from the daughters of the Canaanites, among whom I live, but you will go to my country and to my relatives, and take a wife for my son Isaac." (Genesis 24:1-4)

Now, the consent of the bride-to-be must be an essential consideration. Rebecca is an example of how, when the servant of Abraham asked to marry his son, Isaac, she went willingly.

"And they said, "We will call the girl and consult her wishes." Then they called Rebekah and said to her, "Will you go with this man?" And she said, "I will go." Thus they sent away their sister Rebekah and her nurse with Abraham's servant and his men." (Genesis 24:57-59)

When it comes to negotiating in marriage, there is a Hebrew word called the *Mohar*, where the groom's and bride's father must negotiate in the Jewish wedding contract. In Genesis, Abraham's servant brought out articles of silver and gold and garments and gave them to Rebekah (see Genesis 24:52–53). *Mattan* was a Hebrew word for the gifts given by the groom to the bride in addition to the *Mohar.* The Bible doesn't specify what was to be done with the mohar in case either party broke the marriage agreement of the two parties. [2]

We cannot be made to have a connection with Jesus any more than we can be made to be in a relationship with someone else. Rather, the Holy Spirit inquires of us whether we are prepared to follow Jesus and make a loving commitment to Him. This is akin to the way God chose us by sending His Son to die, be buried, and then rise from the dead. The Holy Spirit approaches us as if He were a matchmaker, asking whether we want to give our lives to Jesus and marry. In a separate water rite known as the Mikvahm, which represents spiritual purification, the bride and groom participate in the betrothal, a premarital ceremony. Jesus had gone through the same thing when John the Baptist baptized Him:

Then Jesus *arrived from Galilee at the Jordan, coming to John to be baptized by him. But John tried to prevent Him, saying, "I have need to be baptized by You, and do You come to me?" But Jesus answering said to him, "Permit it at this time; for in this way it is fitting for us to fulfill all righteousness." Then he *permitted Him. After being baptized, Jesus came up immediately from the water; and behold, the heavens were opened, and he saw the Spirit of God descending as a dove and lighting on Him, and behold, a voice out of the heavens said, "This is My beloved Son, in whom I am well-pleased." (Matthew 3:13-17).

Jesus also said that those who have believed and been baptized shall be saved, but those who disbelieved shall be condemned. (See Mark 16:16.) Jesus underwent a water baptism to symbolize purification before the betrothal. Similarly, believers receive spiritual cleansing through grace and faith before their betrothal with Christ. Our water baptism serves as an external representation of our internal reality.

The Engagement Period: Spiritual Preparation and the Symbolism of the Ring

In a traditional Jewish wedding ceremony, the next significant step is known as "Erusin" or "Kiddushin." During this sacred moment, the groom presents the bride with a ring or another valuable item to symbolize his commitment to marry her. Legally, this act establishes their marital union, yet they cannot live together as husband and wife. This engagement period can extend for up to a year, during which the bride diligently prepares for married life. Various rituals may be observed during this time, including the reading of Psalms, as the couple seeks to strengthen their emotional and spiritual purity before embarking on their journey as a married couple. It beautifully underscores the significance of spiritual and emotional preparation and emphasizes the role of communal support and celebration within the wedding process.

The symbol of the ring holds a profound connection to the essence of the gospel. The bride is reminded of her union with her beloved groom whenever she gazes upon her hand. In times when the bride is physically absent or occupied with preparations, a mere glance at the ring brings her back to the reality of their bond. Similarly, as believers, we have the privilege of beholding the Bridegroom's imminent return, for the Holy Spirit seals us. This seal serves as a constant reminder of our connection to Christ, even in His physical absence. It assures us of His faithfulness and stirs our hope as we eagerly anticipate His glorious return.

Just as the ring represents the unbreakable bond between a bride and groom, the sealing of the Holy Spirit symbolizes our eternal union with Christ. It is a reminder of our identity as His chosen bride, filling us with anticipation and joy as we await His triumphant arrival.

"In Him, you also, after listening to the message of truth, the gospel of your salvation—having also believed, you were sealed in Him with the Holy Spirit of promise, which is given as a pledge

of our inheritance, with a view to the redemption of God's own possession, to the praise of His glory." (Ephesians 1:13-14)

And:

"Now He who prepared us for this very purpose is God, who gave to us the Spirit as a pledge." (2 Corinthians 5:5). Jesus has given us the Holy Spirit as a deposit to remind us of His imminent return!

Notice how the bride and the groom are never together. Yet, they have made a covenant to be reunited in marriage eventually. In the same way, we are married to Jesus and waiting for His return to claim us. One of my favorite passages in the Bible is the parable of the ten virgins. Jesus explained in this parable that these ten virgins were believers, but there were five wise and five foolish. All had oil, and this passage talks about the stewardship of the Lord and how their outcome determines their relationship with the Lord. Most notable in this work of the bridegroom is that someone shouts out to the bridegroom for returning!

"Then the kingdom of heaven will be comparable to ten virgins, who took their lamps and went out to meet the bridegroom. Five of them were foolish, and five were prudent. For when the foolish took their lamps, they took no oil with them, but the prudent took oil in flasks along with their lamps. Now, while the bridegroom was delaying, they all got drowsy and began to sleep. But at midnight, there was a shout, 'Behold, the bridegroom! Come out to meet him.' Then, all those virgins rose and trimmed their lamps. The foolish said to the prudent, 'Give us some of your oil, for our lamps are going out.' But the

prudent answered, 'No, there will not be enough for us and you too; go instead to the dealers and buy some for yourselves.' And while they were going away to make the purchase, the bridegroom came, and those who were ready went in with him to the wedding feast, and the door was shut. Later, the other virgins also came, saying, 'Lord, lord, open up for us.' But he answered, 'Truly I say to you, I do not know you.' Be on the alert then, for you do not know the day nor the hour." (Matthew 25:1-13)

Jesus explains that believers need to be ready and prepared for His return to come to claim us as His bride. You cannot start a wedding ceremony without looking spotless, especially when a bride wears her dirty white dress.

The Nissuin: A Symbolic Unification and Anticipation of Christ's Return

The last order in the Jewish wedding ceremony is the "Nissuin," also known as the "chuppah," or wedding canopy. During this stage, the bride is brought back home, and the couple is officially considered married according to Jewish law. The ceremony is usually held under a canopy, which symbolizes the new home that the couple will create together. Friends and family celebrate by reciting blessings, breaking the glass to remember the temple's destruction in Jerusalem, and joining the joyful festivities.

"If I go and prepare a place for you, I will come again and receive you to Myself, that where I am, there you may be also." (John 14:3)

In the same way, Jesus comes back as Bridegroom and has gone to prepare a place for us. He is coming back soon! He is coming back like a thief in the night.

"But the day of the Lord will come like a thief, in which the heavens will pass away with a roar, the elements will be destroyed with intense heat, and the earth and its works will be burned up." (2 Peter 3:10)

Not only is Jesus our Bridegroom, but He is also a Judge who will come and judge the living and the dead. As for the bride, for those who believe in Jesus, it's essential to live a life that is consecrated, holy, and pure in preparation of the Nissuin and the Wedding Feast of the Lamb, when the Groom comes with the blast of the shofar to bring His Bride home. (see 1 Thessalonians 4:16). This is an old Jewish wedding custom; now, in modern Judaism, the Erusin and Nissuin are combined into one.

"Then I saw a new heaven and a new earth; for the first heaven and the first earth passed away, and there is no longer any sea. And I saw the holy city, new Jerusalem, coming down out of heaven from God, made ready as a bride adorned for her husband." (Revelation 21:1-2)

When Jesus returns, we are reunited with Him and celebrate the Lamb's marriage supper. Unfortunately, there will be those who won't share the celebration with Him because they don't know Him! We're currently in the Erusin period before the Bridegroom comes back!

"Behold, I am coming quickly, and My reward is with Me, to render to every man according to what he has done." (Revelation 22:12)

"The Spirit and the bride say, "Come." And let the one who hears say, "Come." And let the one who is thirsty come; let the one who wishes take the water of life without cost." (Revelation 22:17) And after He finished everything, He will be crowned as King.

"So that at the name of Jesus every knee will bow, of those who are in heaven and on earth and under the earth, and that every tongue will confess that Jesus Christ is Lord, to the glory of God the Father." (Philippians 2:10-11)

Conclusion

It has been a journey; I want to thank you and honor your time reading this book. The purpose of this book is to submit to His Lordship and become disciples of Jesus. The entire world must hear the Truth, which is Jesus Christ. As you continue on your journey with God, please put your faith in Him regardless of what it looks like to you. Whether it seems like you're in a waiting season or not, Abraham had never wavered in belief for twenty-five years before Isaac came around. By simply beholding Jesus and His finished works on the cross, we can continue to strive for His rest.

"For the one who has entered His rest has himself also rested from his works, as God did from His. Therefore, let us be diligent to enter that rest, so that no one will fall, through following the same example of disobedience." (Hebrews 4:11).

You have been given the inheritance of the Father (see Ephesians 1:11), and Christ has fulfilled the work on your behalf. As you read through the scriptures, know that God's intention with you isn't to receive the knowledge of the Word simply but the power of the Word. John 1 says that in the beginning was the Word, God was the Word, and He is the Word made in the flesh. Jesus has been given authority above every principality, power, authority, and dominion so that you can acknowledge the seven confessions of the faith and simply behold His finished works on the cross. I encourage you to go deep and invite the precious Holy Spirit everywhere. In Greek, the word 'filled' in transliteration is plēróō, which, in Thayer's definition, is to be made full, filled up, supplied, and complete. The word filled is taken from Ephesians 5:18: *"Do not get drunk on wine, which leads to debauchery. Instead, be filled with the Spirit."* [3]

It is of utmost importance that we diligently live out the timeless principles and teachings found within Scripture, harmonizing our lives with God's divine will and purpose. Our faith must remain firmly rooted in the unchanging truth of God's Word, and we should seek the guidance of the Holy Spirit, who graciously reveals the profound depths of its wisdom. Through Jesus' sacrificial act, He has taken the weight of our sins upon Himself, enabling us to receive His righteousness as a gift. It is not something we earn through our efforts; rather, it is received by faith. Walking in righteousness positions us exactly where God intends us to be, aligning us with His perfect plan. [4]

May this journey of exploration and discovery ignite a deeper love for the Lord within our hearts, compelling us to walk in righteousness as a natural outpouring of our faith. Let it serve as a constant reminder for us to remain faithful and watchful, eagerly anticipating the glorious return of our Bridegroom, Jesus Christ. As we delve into the wisdom and insights gleaned from these ancient traditions, may we apply them practically to our lives, propelling us forward in our pursuit of God's Kingdom.

In closing, let us remember the words of the psalmist: *"Teach me your way, Lord, that I may rely on your faithfulness;*

---

[3] Ancient Jewish Wedding Customs and Yeshua's Second Coming." Free.Messianicbible.Com, free.messianicbible.com/feature/ancient-jewish-wedding-customs-and-yeshuas-second-coming/.

[4] Schauss, Hayyim . "Ancient Jewish Marriage." My Jewish Learning, www.myjewishlearning.com/article/ancient-jewish-marriage/.

give me an undivided heart, that I may fear your name" (see Psalm 86:11).

May this prayer be on our lips as we continue to journey deeper into the richness of our faith, embracing the blessings and challenges that come with it. May we be transformed by the truth and grace of our Lord Jesus Christ, living as His faithful and devoted disciples until the day of His glorious return. Amen.

Citations

1. "Ancient Jewish Wedding Customs and Yeshua's Second Coming." Free Messianic Bible, free.messianicbible.com/feature/ancient-jewish-wedding-customs-and-yeshuas-second-coming/.

2. Schauss, Hayyim. "Ancient Jewish Marriage." My Jewish Learning, www.myjewishlearning.com/article/ancient-jewish-marriage/.

3. Lewis, C.S. Mere Christianity. Geoffrey Bles, 1952, p. 69.

4. Houzel, Suzana H. "The Remarkable, yet Not Extraordinary, Human Brain As a Scaled-up Primate Brain and Its Associated Cost." Proceedings of the National Academy of Sciences (PNAS), 22 Jun. 2012.

Made in United States
Troutdale, OR
10/18/2024

23905281R00137